JOHNNIE COCHRAN

❧

DATE DUE

RHW17			
Bid			
PM1			
TC2			

JOHNNIE COCHRAN

❧

Cookie Lommel

CHELSEA HOUSE PUBLISHERS
Philadelphia

8087
ACF-7085

Chelsea House Publishers

Editor in Chief	Stephen Reginald
Production Manager	Pamela Loos
Director of Photography	Judy L. Hasday
Art Director	Sara Davis
Managing Editor	James D. Gallagher
Senior Production Editor	LeeAnne Gelletly

Staff for JOHNNIE COCHRAN

Project Editor	James D. Gallagher
Associate Art Director	Takeshi Takahashi
Designer	21st Century Publishing and Communications
Picture Researcher	Patricia Burns
Cover Designer	Emiliano Begnardi
Cover photos	AP/Wide World Photos

© 2000 by Chelsea House Publishers, a division of Main Line Book Co. All rights reserved. Printed and bound in the United States of America.

The Chelsea House World Wide Web address is
http://www.chelseahouse.com

First Printing

1 3 5 7 9 8 6 4 2

Library of Congress Cataloging-in-Publication Data

Lommel, Cookie.
Johnnie Cochran / by Cookie Lommel
      p.   cm. —(Black Americans of Achievement)
Includes bibliographical references and index.
Summary: A biography of the lawyer who successfully defended O. J. Simpson in one of the most famous trials of the century.
ISBN 0-7910-5279-6 (hc). — ISBN 0-7910-5280-X (pb)
1. Cochran, Johnnie 1937–   —Juvenile literature. 2. Afro-American lawyers—California—Biography—Juvenile literature. [1. Cochran, Johnnie, 1937–   . 2. Lawyers. 3. Afro-Americans—Biography.] I. Title. II. Series.
KF373.C59L66   1999
340'.092—dc21
[B]   99–31424
                                                                          CIP

Frontis: Johnnie Cochran built a reputation as an advocate for African Americans and has become one of the best defense attorneys in America today.

CONTENTS

BLACK AMERICANS OF ACHIEVEMENT

HENRY AARON
baseball great

KAREEM ABDUL-JABBAR
basketball great

MUHAMMAD ALI
heavyweight champion

RICHARD ALLEN
*religious leader and
social activist*

MAYA ANGELOU
author

LOUIS ARMSTRONG
musician

ARTHUR ASHE
tennis great

JOSEPHINE BAKER
entertainer

JAMES BALDWIN
author

TYRA BANKS
model

BENJAMIN BANNEKER
scientist and mathematician

AMIRI BARAKA
poet and playwright

COUNT BASIE
bandleader and composer

ROMARE BEARDEN
artist

JAMES BECKWOURTH
frontiersman

MARY McLEOD BETHUNE
educator

GEORGE WASHINGTON
CARVER
botanist

CHARLES CHESNUTT
author

JOHNNIE COCHRAN
lawyer

BILL COSBY
entertainer

PAUL CUFFE
merchant and abolitionist

MILES DAVIS
musician

FATHER DIVINE
religious leader

FREDERICK DOUGLASS
abolitionist editor

CHARLES DREW
physician

W. E. B. DU BOIS
scholar and activist

PAUL LAURENCE DUNBAR
poet

DUKE ELLINGTON
bandleader and composer

RALPH ELLISON
author

JULIUS ERVING
basketball great

LOUIS FARRAKHAN
political activist

ELLA FITZGERALD
singer

MORGAN FREEMAN
actor

MARCUS GARVEY
black nationalist leader

JOSH GIBSON
baseball great

WHOOPI GOLDBERG
entertainer

CUBA GOODING JR.
actor

ALEX HALEY
author

PRINCE HALL
social reformer

JIMI HENDRIX
musician

MATTHEW HENSON
explorer

GREGORY HINES
performer

BILLIE HOLIDAY
singer

LENA HORNE
entertainer

WHITNEY HOUSTON
singer and actress

LANGSTON HUGHES
poet

ZORA NEALE HURSTON
author

JANET JACKSON
singer

JESSE JACKSON
civil-rights leader and politician

MICHAEL JACKSON
entertainer

SAMUEL L. JACKSON
actor

T. D. JAKES
religious leader

JACK JOHNSON
heavyweight champion

MAGIC JOHNSON
basketball great

SCOTT JOPLIN
composer

BARBARA JORDAN
politician

MICHAEL JORDAN
basketball great

CORETTA SCOTT KING
civil-rights leader

MARTIN LUTHER KING JR.
civil-rights leader

LEWIS LATIMER
scientist

SPIKE LEE
filmmaker

CARL LEWIS
champion athlete

JOE LOUIS
heavyweight champion

RONALD MCNAIR
astronaut

MALCOLM X
militant black leader

BOB MARLEY
musician

THURGOOD MARSHALL
Supreme Court justice

TONI MORRISON
author

ELIJAH MUHAMMAD
religious leader

EDDIE MURPHY
entertainer

JESSE OWENS
champion athlete

SATCHEL PAIGE
baseball great

CHARLIE PARKER
musician

ROSA PARKS
civil-rights leader

COLIN POWELL
military leader

PAUL ROBESON
singer and actor

JACKIE ROBINSON
baseball great

CHRIS ROCK
comedian/actor

DIANA ROSS
entertainer

WILL SMITH
actor

CLARENCE THOMAS
Supreme Court justice

SOJOURNER TRUTH
antislavery activist

HARRIET TUBMAN
antislavery activist

NAT TURNER
slave revolt leader

TINA TURNER
entertainer

DENMARK VESEY
slave revolt leader

ALICE WALKER
author

MADAM C. J. WALKER
entrepreneur

BOOKER T. WASHINGTON
educator

DENZEL WASHINGTON
actor

J. C. WATTS
politician

VANESSA WILLIAMS
singer and actress

OPRAH WINFREY
entertainer

TIGER WOODS
golf star

RICHARD WRIGHT
author

ON
ACHIEVEMENT

Coretta Scott King

BEFORE YOU BEGIN this book, I hope you will ask yourself what the word *excellence* means to you. I think it's a question we should all ask, and keep asking as we grow older and change. Because the truest answer to it should never change. When you think of excellence, perhaps you think of success at work; or of becoming wealthy; or meeting the right person, getting married, and having a good family life.

Those goals are worth striving for, but there is a better way to look at excellence. As Martin Luther King Jr. said in one of his last sermons, "I want you to be first in love. I want you to be first in moral excellence. I want you to be first in generosity. If you want to be important, wonderful. If you want to be great, wonderful. But recognize that he who is greatest among you shall be your servant."

My husband knew that the true meaning of achievement is service. When I met him, in 1952, he was already ordained as a Baptist minister and was working toward a doctoral degree at Boston University. I was studying at the New England Conservatory and dreamed of accomplishments in music. We married a year later, and after I graduated the following year we moved to Montgomery, Alabama. We didn't know it then, but our notions of achievement were about to undergo a dramatic change.

You may have read or heard about what happened next. What began with the boycott of a local bus line grew into a national crusade, and by the time he was assassinated in 1968 my husband had fashioned a black movement powerful enough to shatter forever the practice of racial segregation. What you may not have read about is where he learned to resist injustice without compromising his religious beliefs.

He adopted a strategy of nonviolence from a man of a different race, who lived in a different country and even practiced a different religion. The man was Mahatma Gandhi, the great leader of India, who devoted his life to serving humanity in the spirit of love and nonviolence. It was in these principles that Martin discovered his method for social reform. More than anything else, those two principles were the key to his achievements.

These books are about African Americans who served society through the excellence of their achievements. They form part of the rich history of black men and women in America—a history of stunning accomplishments in every field of human endeavor, from literature and art to science, industry, education, diplomacy, athletics, jurisprudence, even polar exploration.

Not all of the people in this history had the same ideals, but I think you will find that all of them had something in common. Like Martin Luther King Jr., they all decided to become "drum majors" and serve humanity. In that principle—whether it was expressed in books, inventions, or song—they found a goal and a guide outside themselves that showed them a way to serve others instead of living only for themselves.

Reading the stories of these courageous men and women not only helps us discover the principles that we will use to guide our own lives; it also teaches us about our black heritage and about America itself. It is crucial for us to know the heroes and heroines of our history and to realize that the price we paid in our struggle for equality in America was dear. But we must also understand that we have gotten as far as we have partly because America's democratic system and ideals made it possible.

We are still struggling with racism and prejudice. But the great men and women in this series are a tribute to the spirit of the country in which they have flourished. And that makes their stories special and worth knowing.

1

BEGINNING A JOURNEY TO JUSTICE

❧

THE ELEGANT-LOOKING African-American attorney wore a designer suit with a simple cross pinned to his lapel as he stood outside the building that housed the Orange County Superior Court. It was a cool June day in California, with winds blowing in from the Pacific Ocean just a few miles away. But the man didn't allow the wind to ruffle his composure. Very few things could. As a consequence, he always looked professional and in control. Johnnie L. Cochran Jr. was one of the best-known lawyers in the country. Very few lawyers were anxious to face this man's confident, smooth style in the courtroom.

Today, Cochran and his partner, Stuart Hanlon, were the last hope for a long-imprisoned man named Elmer "Geronimo" Pratt. He had been jailed for murder 25 years earlier, but had always contended that he was innocent. Pratt had tried to obtain a new trial five times, and had applied for parole 16 times. All requests had been denied. This was his sixth attempt to overturn his 1972 murder conviction.

Johnnie Cochran Jr. was prepared for his role. As a young lawyer, he had dedicated his life to the pursuit of justice for people who were not well represented in the American courts. When Cochran began his career in Los Angeles during the turbulent 1960s, minorities, especially African Americans, could not expect fair treatment from every police officer every time they

Johnnie L. Cochran Jr. exhibits his cool outside a California court building. On June 10, 1997, outside the Orange County Courthouse, he hoped that a 25-year-old injustice would finally be righted.

came to the notice of the law. Johnnie Cochran understood the difficulties faced by minorities, and wanted to change this unequal situation. It was this commitment that brought him to the Orange County Superior Court on June 10, 1997, as he waited to see if Pratt would finally be released on bail.

Pratt's identity had been a crucial part of his 1972 conviction. A former munitions expert for the U.S. military, he had been wounded twice while serving in Vietnam. When Pratt returned to the United States, he became angered by the unfair treatment of African Americans. Pratt joined a militant political group called the Black Panthers, eventually becoming the leader of the Los Angeles Panther organization. The Black Panthers advocated violence in order to achieve equal rights for African Americans. Because of this, the federal government kept a close eye on Panther activities, and the group was infiltrated by members of the Federal Bureau of Investigation (FBI).

On December 18, 1968, two young African-American men robbed and shot a couple playing tennis in Santa Monica, California. Kenneth Olsen survived the brutal attack, but his wife, Caroline, was killed. The police had several suspects, but in December 1970 they arrested Pratt, charging him with the murder. Although Pratt claimed that he had been nearly 400 miles away, attending a meeting of Black Panther leaders in Oakland at the time of the killing, the jury found him guilty on the basis of what they were told by the prosecutor, deputy district attorney Richard Kalustian. In 1972 Pratt was sentenced to life in prison.

The ruling was a shock to Pratt's young lawyer—Johnnie Cochran. He had been positive that Pratt was innocent and would be released. "I felt we were going to win because I knew we were right," Cochran later said.

After Pratt's conviction, Cochran discovered new evidence that showed the police had illegally concealed information about their star witness, an informant named Julius Butler. Other evidence that might have helped

Pratt's defense had mysteriously disappeared. However, the jailed activist could not get a new trial. Cochran came to believe, like many others, that Pratt had been framed for the awful murder of Caroline Olsen. Cochran blamed a corrupt legal system for what he considered a terrible error, and vowed that he would never rest until the verdict was overturned and his client released.

The lawyer continued to press the court on Pratt's behalf, and in 1996 Gilbert Garcetti, the district attorney of Los Angeles, finally agreed to take a new look at the evidence. By then, Elmer "Geronimo" Pratt had been in prison in northern California for over 25 years. Although Garcetti, like his predecessors in the district attorney's office, did not think that the evidence warranted a new trial, Cochran insisted on a hearing. Judge Everett Dickey of the Superior Court would preside over the hearing on June 10, 1997.

The courtroom was tense. People who could not

Cochran makes a point during a hearing for Elmer "Geronimo" Pratt, who is seated at the right. For over 25 years, the attorney fought to overturn Pratt's 1972 murder conviction. Cochran argued that the case against his client was persecution because Pratt had been a member of the Black Panthers, and that important evidence had been suppressed at the original trial.

squeeze themselves inside the packed courtroom were forced to line the hallways and the outside of the courthouse. Many had come to support Pratt, including some fellow activists. One was David Hilliard, a founder of the Black Panthers, who now said that he believed Pratt had been framed by police and the FBI. Ironically, Hilliard had refused to testify at Pratt's original trial because of a division in the Black Panther party's leadership. This had weakened Pratt's alibi. But Hilliard was here for Pratt now.

As Pratt, wearing a yellow prison jumpsuit, spoke to the judge, his voice was hoarse with emotion. He promised to follow the court's direction if his 1972 conviction was overturned and he was released on bail pending a retrial. "I assure you that if there are any further proceedings, I'll be the first one here," said Pratt. "You can be assured I will adhere to any rule the court orders me to follow and that's my word as a Vietnam vet and a man."

Pratt's lawyers argued that the case was actually about setting limits on the powers of government in a free society. Pratt, they said, had been "railroaded" by the FBI as part of an effort to destroy the Black Panther movement. The Los Angeles County district attorney's office wanted Pratt's conviction maintained. Prosecutors also argued that even if the judge should order a new trial, the former Black Panther should not be released from prison on bail. Excitement rose among the spectators. How would Judge Dickey rule, to release this man or to return him to prison?

As the two sides reviewed the evidence for Judge Dickey, the case became clearer. The prosecutors reiterated their evidence from the original trial. Pratt's car, a GTO convertible with North Carolina registration, had been seen at the scene of the murder. Pratt's gun, a .45 automatic, had been used to commit the horrendous killing.

Cochran attempted to provoke a reasonable doubt in the judge's mind about whether the FBI, the Los Angeles police department, and the district attorney's office had followed proper procedures during the original trial to ensure that the physical evidence was untainted and that all relevant facts were presented. He pointed out that many times during the 1972 Pratt trial, appropriate procedures had not been followed or evidence had been suppressed.

Johnnie was particularly upset about one of the key pieces of evidence used to convict Pratt, a confession that the Black Panther allegedly made to Julius Butler. Butler was an informant for the FBI who had infiltrated the Black Panther party. During Pratt's original trial, Butler had lied in court when asked if he had a relationship with law officials that could prevent his testimony from being regarded as impartial. He said that he had never before worked as an informant.

Cochran had not known in 1972 that Butler was lying. The young attorney believed that he was given the truthful details of the case as was required legally and ethically. But now Cochran knew, thanks to an investigator hired in 1980 by the defense to find information that would lead to a retrial, that Julius Butler had informed for the FBI at least 30 times before the Olsen murder. And Butler had another motive to blame the murder on Pratt: jealousy. Pratt had been selected over the older man for the leadership position of the Los Angeles Black Panthers.

Cochran also informed the judge that Butler was not the only person who claimed to have heard someone confess to killing Caroline Olsen. The Los Angeles Police Department had picked up another man, Black Panther Tyrone Hutchinson, who said that he had overheard two other Black Panthers, Herbert Swilley and Larry Hatter, admit to the crime. However, this information had never been brought to light during the first trial. Hutchinson said that he had failed to reveal this confession during the 1972 Pratt trial because the police had threatened his life.

The defense also attacked the testimony of Kenneth Olsen, who in 1972 had identified Pratt as the killer. At the time, Olsen's testimony was believed to be infallible. But now the defense pointed out that Olsen had lied to

Free at last: Geronimo Pratt celebrates his release on bail pending a retrial with his daughter, Shona. Johnnie Cochran is standing at Pratt's right.

the jury. During the original trial, Olsen indicated that Pratt was the only man he identified as the attacker, leaving no room for reasonable doubt. However Larry Rivetz, a Los Angeles public defender who heard of this testimony after Pratt's conviction, knew that this statement was wrong. His own client, Ronald Perkins, had been identified by Kenneth Olsen as the murderer in a police lineup before Pratt was charged. Because Perkins had been in prison at the time of the slaying, he could not have committed the crime, so he was released. Mysteriously, the lineup card that showed Olsen's false identification had disappeared from police files, and during the 1972 trial Johnnie Cochran did not know the card existed. Now he made sure that Judge Dickey knew what had been concealed from the defense and the jury 25 years earlier.

An ugly picture of a terrible crime against Pratt was

emerging. Although the Black Panthers had been involved in violence, the unethical conduct of the police and the FBI was unsettling. Cochran had built his career on the belief that the integrity of officials who represent the law must be unimpeachable. This principle had been his guide during the case of Ron Settles, an African-American football player wrongfully killed by a police choke hold, and during Cochran's lawsuit against a police officer who repeatedly assaulted a young Latino girl sexually. It was his light in the suit of Leonard Deadwyler's bereaved family, who protested the "accidental" killing of this unarmed man by police, and may have been a motivation for his unrelenting pursuit of policeman Mark Fuhrman during the notorious O. J. Simpson trial.

And now, in the Orange County courtroom, Johnnie Cochran's focus on the integrity of law enforcement in the case of Elmer Pratt was about to be rewarded. After all the evidence was presented, Judge Everett Dickey ordered that the district attorney either give Pratt a new trial or drop the charges. And then he gave the order that Pratt had been dreaming of for over 25 years in a grim prison cell northeast of San Francisco: he agreed to free Pratt on bail until the new trial could be organized. For the first time in a quarter of a century, Elmer Pratt would be released from prison.

Screams of joy and clapping ricocheted down the courthouse walls and outside. Jubilant supporters chanted and cheered. Pratt, who in prison had changed his name to Geronimo ji Jaga, addressed the judge. "Thank you from the bottom of my heart for your fair and courageous ruling," Pratt said, hugging his daughter, who was graduating from high school that afternoon. He told the throng of news reporters that his first priority as a free man on bail was to visit his 94-year-old mother in Louisiana. At 12:35 P.M., amidst shouts of "free at last, free at last, thank God almighty, he's free at last," Geronimo ji Jaga walked out of the dark courtroom into the June sun, a free man. Johnnie Cochran, too, was free at last, a 25-year-old burden lifted from his shoulders.

2

AN ADVOCATE
IN THE MAKING

— ❦ —

JOHNNIE COCHRAN'S GRANDFATHER, Alonso "Lonnie" Crockrum, had been born on a cotton plantation in Caddo Parish, Louisiana, in the late 19th century. He changed the family name from Crockrum to Cochran, because he felt that the simpler version might get him further in the world.

Alonso and his wife Hannah were sharecroppers; they raised six acres of cotton on a plantation that was owned by four brothers, white men named Hutchinson. Sharecropping was a common practice in the South after the Civil War. Landowners would allow farmers to live on the land and grow crops. The farmers would be given seed and farm tools to work the land. When the crops were harvested, the owner would take a percentage of the value as rent for land and tools, and the farmers would keep the little money that remained.

After the cotton was harvested, the Hutchinsons gave the Cochrans their share of the proceeds from the sale of the crop. However, the payment was in credit that could only be used at a general store owned by the Hutchinsons.

When Hannah Cochran gave birth to a child in 1917, Lonnie was determined that his son, Johnnie, would have opportunities that had eluded African Americans before him. Lonnie saved his money to buy books and insisted that his son follow a routine of

A view of the main street of Shreveport, Louisiana, where Johnnie L. Cochran Jr. was born in 1937.

19

Johnnie Cochran's grandparents were sharecroppers, who rented and farmed land in exchange for a share of the profit from the crops. This was a common arrangement in the South after the Civil War. This photo shows how black tenant farmers often worked together to help each other.

work and study. After a full day in school, Johnnie would help out in the field and then spend the rest of the day reading, either by daylight or after dark by kerosene lamplight.

By the time he was a young teenager, Johnnie had exhausted all the educational resources that Caddo Parish had to offer him, so Lonnie and Hannah sent their son 20 miles north to live in Shreveport, Louisiana, with Hannah's younger sister, Lucille, and her husband. Many other African Americans had moved to that area, because Shreveport had one of the few high schools for black students.

Johnnie took the entrance examinations at Central Colored High and passed them with such high marks that he was admitted to the 10th grade. He thrived at

Central, soon becoming the top student in his class. Although he had to return home twice a year to help with the spring planting and fall harvest, he planned to go to college as his father wished. Those plans were canceled, though, when Lonnie died in 1935 after a botched operation to relieve a bleeding ulcer.

Johnnie returned home to bring in his parents' cotton crop. The 400 pounds of cotton that he picked each day was enough to pay off the Cochran family's debt to the Hutchinsons. He then took his mother to Shreveport. The 18-year-old and his cousin, Arthur Lee, rented a house where they could live with Hannah Cochran and Lee's widowed mother. However, although Johnnie was a high school graduate, the only job he could find was as a drugstore delivery boy.

While at Central Colored High, Johnnie had fallen in love with a quiet young woman named Hattie Bass. She shared his determination to get ahead, as well as his deep religious convictions. After graduation she had returned to her parents' home about 10 miles outside of Shreveport.

Hattie's parents, Emmanuel and Cloteal Bass, owned their own farm, which had thick groves of pine trees and fields of bamboo and sugar cane. Emmanuel was a renowned entrepreneur in Caddo Parish. Although he was well known for growing the largest watermelon crop in the area, much of his income came from his skill as a tree surgeon and from his development of more productive strains of the southern pecan tree. Emmanuel Bass was also a highly respected community and religious leader.

Soon after Johnnie returned to Shreveport, he and Hattie Bass were married. On October 2, 1937, Hattie gave birth to their first child. They named the boy Johnnie L. Cochran Jr. He would eventually have two sisters, Pearl and Martha Jean, and a brother, RaLonzo.

Johnnie was born during the Great Depression, a time when even the people fortunate enough to have jobs found it hard to survive financially. Soon after Johnnie Jr.'s birth, his father took a job selling insurance for the Louisiana Industrial Insurance Company. Johnnie Sr. liked the insurance business. It appealed to his entrepreneurial spirit, while giving him a way to help those around him.

Johnnie Cochran Jr. grew up in a rented three-bedroom house with his grandmother, his father's cousin Arthur, and Arthur's mother, whom Johnnie Jr. called Aunt Easter. His childhood was filled with warm hugs, words of encouragement, and his mother's wonderful cooking.

Sundays were memorable days for the Cochran family. The Little Union Baptist Church was just a block away from their home in Shreveport's Lakeside section. Johnnie's grandmother sang in the choir, and his young father was a deacon. The family walked to the church together, and conversed with neighborhood friends along the way. In the afternoons, the family often drove out to the Bass farm. At dinner, they would talk about the lessons discussed in church.

Although Johnnie's father was just in his twenties, his faith and compassion led people in the community to solicit his advice. He was also fond of composing helpful aphorisms similar to those of the Greek philosophers, whom he learned to appreciate while he was in high school. Sunday dinners were not complete without Johnnie Sr. telling his children, "Always recognize that all human endeavors are imperfect and incomplete." But this did not mean that he wanted his children to reach for lesser goals. Johnnie Sr. often reminded his family, "Perfection demands continuous study, growth, progress and change," and "Good deeds enhance the worth of each individual while evil deeds destroy or bankrupt the lives of all who engage in them."

Johnnie's mother, not to be outdone by her husband, offered the children her own pearls of wisdom: "Always be the best that you can be," and "The truth crushed to the earth will rise again." This notion of truth's

inherent power stuck with Johnnie and his siblings.

Johnnie Jr. was also influenced by the pastor of the Baptist church, C. A. W. Clark. The small but strict preacher often exhorted his congregation to give of themselves in order to receive. In his 1996 autobiography *Journey to Justice*, Cochran remembered that Pastor Clark was fond of quoting James 2:17, "Faith, if it hath not works, is dead."

Although life in Louisiana was often difficult for African Americans during the 1930s and '40s, young Johnnie and his sisters were not always aware of segregation. When he went to a movie on a Saturday,

The Little Union Baptist Church in Shreveport was just a block away from the Cochran home. Johnnie Cochran Sr. was a deacon at the church, and Hannah Cochran, Johnnie Jr.'s grandmother, sang in the choir.

Johnnie Cochran Jr., as a young attorney, with his father. Johnnie Sr., an insurance salesman, always pushed his children to improve themselves.

Johnnie Jr. wasn't upset that blacks didn't have free access to all areas of the segregated theaters. He remembers simply accepting his relegation to the balcony because he was expected to do so. The only white person he really knew as a child was the daughter of the family for whom his grandmother did housework. There were no white children in his school, and he never questioned why.

In 1942, the Cochran family's lives would change dramatically. The United States had entered World War II. Because Johnnie Sr. had to support his wife, three young children, and his mother, he could not enter military service. Still, he wanted to contribute to the country's battle overseas. When he learned that there were unfilled jobs for "the war effort" in California, he listened intently. In the shipyards on the West Coast, black and white men worked side by side for the same wages. "A man always has to be going for something better," Lonnie Cochran had always said, and his son knew it would be hard to find as good an opportunity in Louisiana. Hattie helped make his decision easier by envisioning a better future for her family in California. In September 1942, the Cochrans left Shreveport and moved to San Francisco.

California's population had been less than 10 million in December 1941, when the Japanese bombed Pearl Harbor and pushed the United States into the war. The state's economy was based mainly on agriculture and shipping, serving as a destination point for raw materials sent into and out of the country. The Second World War, however, changed that. California's shipbuilding, aircraft production, steel, and munitions industries grew enormously. At the same time, food production went into high gear. California's employers needed workers, and no one cared if they were white, black, or Latino. Rural blacks and poor whites from the South and Midwest poured into the shipyards and aircraft factories. Many thousands of Mexican immigrants journeyed northward to work in the fields of the great central and Coachella valleys.

Within a few weeks, Johnnie Sr. found work as a pipefitter with Bethlehem Steel in the Alameda Naval Shipyards. Because San Francisco was bulging at the seams with newcomers, creating a severe housing shortage, the family moved in with Johnnie Jr.'s Aunt Lucinda. It was the first time he had lived in an integrated neighborhood, and Johnnie Jr. remembered it to be harmonious.

School in this new neighborhood was an exciting adventure for the Cochran children. Johnnie Jr. was an excellent student, smart enough to skip second grade in the integrated Alameda elementary school. Johnnie Sr. was an ideal role model for his son. Although he came home exhausted from his 12-hour shifts in the shipyard, he spent most evenings reading and studying. Johnnie Sr. had never stopped believing in the importance of education and continual self-improvement.

When the shipyards began to scale back work after the war ended, Johnnie Sr. was recruited as a salesman by Golden State Mutual, California's leading black-owned insurance company. Johnnie Sr. grabbed the opportunity. Within a short time he was the top selling agent for the company in the San Francisco area. His career was thriving, and he received a promotion that took him to the San Diego office. In the fall of 1949, he was promoted again, this time to an important position at the company headquarters in Los Angeles.

Johnnie Jr. settled in quickly at his new school, Mount Vernon Junior High. The diverse student body came from ambitious, upwardly mobile, middle-class families and the schoolwork was challenging. Still, he rose to the top of the class. Johnnie Jr. also showed a flair for discussion and debate.

Johnnie had many hobbies outside of school. One of his favorites was baseball. He was especially excited in 1947, when Jackie Robinson became the first African American to play major-league baseball. He followed every story about Robinson in the newspapers. Johnnie's father used Jackie Robinson as an example, pointing out that hard work and discipline were necessary to fulfill dreams.

Johnnie Jr. was a hard worker. When he was in junior high he took his first job, running errands and doing chores for a local dry cleaner. Later he was a paperboy, delivering the morning *Los Angeles Herald Examiner*. He also worked with a local catering service that had a large number of affluent customers in Los Angeles.

Shortly after Johnnie Jr. graduated from Mount Vernon Junior High in 1952, his father came home and announced that his son was going to enroll at Los Angeles High School. Even though the Cochrans lived in another high school district, Los Angeles

High was considered the best public school in the city.

Johnnie Sr. and Hattie had always hoped that after finishing high school, their son would study medicine and become a doctor. Instead, Johnnie Jr. informed them that he wanted to be a lawyer. Later he would marvel at the intuition that told him to choose a profession that made such excellent use of his strengths and personal characteristics. "It was like an inner calling," he later said. "Only later would I see how the law had really chosen me, that I was following my destiny."

A highly publicized legal case in 1954, when

With the Japanese attack on Pearl Harbor, and the United States' entry into World War II, the nation's factories went into high gear producing weapons and equipment for the military. Johnnie's father saw an opportunity to take a good job at the Alameda shipyard in California, and moved his family to San Francisco.

*Among Johnnie Cochran Jr.'s childhood heroes were Jackie Robinson (above),
who broke major league baseball's color barrier in 1947, and attorney
Thurgood Marshall (pictured at right). Marshall, flanked by George E. C.
Hayes and James M. Nabrit, argued against segregation of public schools
before the Supreme Court in the landmark 1954 case* Brown v. Board of
Education of Topeka, Kansas. *He eventually would sit on the Supreme
Court himself.*

Johnnie was 17, probably inspired him to pursue the
law as a career. The U.S. Supreme Court's *Brown v.
Board of Education of Topeka, Kansas,* decision
changed public education drastically. It struck down
state laws that allowed segregation of schools. This
meant that African-American students would have the

same educational opportunities as other Americans.
The *Brown v. Board of Education* decision became one
of the significant early moments of the Civil Rights
movement of the 1950s and '60s. The impact of the
ruling on Johnnie Cochran Jr. was great—it confirmed
his decision to become a lawyer and change society

in the same way that the members of the Supreme Court had.

After graduating from high school Johnnie Jr. wanted to go to Harvard, because he wanted to test his abilities against the very best in the country. However, the Cochrans could not afford to pay for a Harvard education and send his sisters to college also. Johnnie Jr. decided to apply to the University of California at Los Angeles (UCLA) instead, and he was accepted.

In his first year, Johnnie Jr. found UCLA intriguing. The student body included many ambitious young adults of all backgrounds. The courses were rigorous and the competition stiff. While he studied, Johnnie also worked for his father. When he turned 18, he had passed the state licensing exam to sell life and disability insurance. As one of 40 agents working under his dad at Golden State Mutual, Johnnie Jr. learned the secrets of the insurance business.

During his senior year at UCLA, Johnnie Jr. met an attractive young woman named Barbara Berry. She had also moved from Shreveport to San Francisco. Both of Barbara's parents were deceased, and she was working her way through college. Soon, they began to date.

When Johnnie graduated from UCLA in the summer of 1959, he decided to attend Loyola Law School. While he would have preferred to stay at UCLA, Loyola had a compact five-day schedule; this would allow him to continue working while attending classes. After his first year of law school, he and Barbara were married.

By his third year at Loyola, Johnnie Jr. had already found work in the legal field. He was hired as the first black law clerk in the office of the Los Angeles city attorney. In Los Angeles, the city attorney and his deputies represent the city government. An elected county official, the district attorney, handles the prosecution of major crimes.

Johnnie Jr. became fascinated by trial work. His supervisors quickly recognized his interest and abilities and assigned him to represent the city in small claims court. From the first day, he won more cases than he lost.

Early in 1962, the young Cochran family's first daughter, Melodie, was born. That June, Johnnie Jr. graduated from law school. However, to become eligible to practice law in California, he had to take a test called the bar examination. Since he had family-size bills to pay, he could not afford to take the exam more than once. It was around this time that Johnnie's car was rear-ended by another driver. This misfortune turned out to be a stroke of good luck. He received a $2,000 settlement from the insurance company, enough to cover his family expenses while he studied intensively for the bar exam.

After he took the bar, he returned to the clerkship with the city attorney, waiting several months for the official results of the test. The pride he felt when he learned he passed the examination was exceeded only by the joy and pride that his parents felt when he told them the news. His father told him that he had never doubted that Johnnie would achieve his goal. His mother choked back tears as she told him how proud she was of what he had accomplished. Within an hour, the news of his success was already a part of the Cochran family legend.

A few weeks later, Johnnie L. Cochran Jr. drove downtown to report for work, this time as a brand new deputy city attorney, fully qualified to practice law in the State of California.

3

THE PROSECUTION

❧

AFTER PASSING THE bar, attorney Johnnie L. Cochran Jr. spent his first three years practicing law as a prosecutor in the Los Angeles city attorney's office. His initial assignments were in traffic court, where he won his first 128 cases. Although the cases didn't have much luster, these early trials helped Johnnie sharpen his prosecutorial techniques.

As he learned how to handle himself in the courtroom, Johnnie also noticed an odd phenomenon. From case to case, Johnnie noticed that the arresting policeman often gave the same "probable cause" story to explain why he pulled over a suspected drunk driver. Before pulling over a motorist, a police officer must have probable cause—in other words, he or she must see some behavior that indicates the driver is intoxicated. Johnnie felt it was odd that nearly all of the suspects in these police accounts allegedly behaved in exactly the same way, exhibiting exactly the demeanor that the law requires for an arrest and conviction on drunk driving charges. Although this made it easy for Cochran to convict drunk drivers, the procedure never sat well with him. He suspected that some of the police officers were lying about the incidents they witnessed.

The Los Angeles Police Department (LAPD) has a long history of corruption and misconduct, dating back to the early 1900s. At that time, businessmen

As a young graduate of the Loyola Law School, Johnnie L. Cochran Jr. wanted to make a difference. But in his first job, as a prosecutor for the city of Los Angeles, Cochran witnessed firsthand discrimination and misuse of police power. Simmering frustration and anger in the African-American community at these injustices finally boiled over in August 1965, causing rioting in the Los Angeles neighborhood of Watts.

When he took over the Los Angeles Police Department, Chief William H. Parker hired officers with military backgrounds. Many of these new hires came from the South or Midwest, where racism was common. Often, innocent blacks of Los Angeles suffered along with the guilty.

and union members were involved in a power struggle. The police department sided with the business owners, often conducting mass arrests of union leaders. The LAPD also became known for its corruption in the 1920s and '30s. During this time, many officers profited from organized crime activities such as bootlegging, gambling, and prostitution. In 1938, a reform movement forced Los Angeles mayor Frank A. Shaw to resign. In a subsequent trial, Shaw's brother was convicted on 66 counts of bribery and of selling city jobs, including positions in the police department.

Even after the reformers took over, the department did not improve much. In his autobiography, Johnnie Cochran commented that the reformers exhibited two major characteristics: a hatred of minorities and a love for big government. And according to Los Angeles historian Kevin Starr, the Los Angeles Police Department became an independent agency as the reformers attempted to clean it up. As the police became more neutral toward labor, they became more vigorous about enforcing racial segregation.

During the post–World War II era, blacks moving to Los Angeles from the segregated South saw racial animosity combined with a new military-style police force that had been introduced by new LAPD chief William Parker. Parker believed that a police force should include former soldiers and marines, who had no connection to the community. Most of these recruits had recently been discharged from military bases in the South and Midwest. When they moved to Los Angeles, they often brought racist attitudes with them.

By 1963, Johnnie's supervisors felt he was ready for more demanding work. Cochran was excited when he received his first important case: the obscenity trial of a comedian named Lenny Bruce.

In the late fifties and early sixties, Bruce had become well-known for his ribald stand-up routines, laced with profanity and racial slurs. To his fans, Bruce was a mastermind in pointing out the hypocrisies in our society in an often blunt and unforgiving manner. For example, in one of his most famous bits he attacked the power of the racial epithet "nigger." The comedian pointed out that attempts to remove the word from people's vocabularies would not erase attitudes of racism and bigotry, and that the taboo against using the word makes it more hurtful when it is used. Removing the stigma attached to the epithet would diminish its ability to bruise the feelings of its intended target, he told audiences. However, the philosophy behind Bruce's stand-up comedy monologues was lost on the Los Angeles Police Department. Bruce was arrested numerous times for obscenity.

One night, vice deputy Sherman Block was dispatched to a club in West Hollywood where Lenny Bruce was performing. Block hid a tape recorder under his shirt and recorded Bruce's obscenity-laced performance. With evidence safely on tape, criminal obscenity charges were filed against Lenny Bruce. Cochran, the department's hot young trial lawyer, was ordered to try the case.

When the tape was played in the courtroom, most of it was inaudible. Only two of Bruce's routines could be understood. The comedian's lawyer, Sydney Irmas, argued that his client was protected by the First Amendment right to freedom of speech. Ultimately, this argument would win the case for Lenny Bruce. Cochran's first celebrity trial was a bust, but he gained a lifelong friend in Syd Irmas, who would eventually try cases with the young lawyer.

Despite the loss in the high-profile Lenny Bruce case, by 1965 Johnnie had become one of the city attorney's top trial lawyers. Many of his cases involved prosecuting people charged with violating Section 148 of the California Penal Code, which prohibits resisting arrest or interfering with an officer in the course of his duties. As Cochran handled more and more of these "148s," he started to see another unsettling pattern. He noticed that the defendants would often show up in court heavily bruised or cut. Some even had fractured limbs. Yet the policemen whom they had allegedly attacked were inexplicably uninjured. Cochran noticed another disturbing trend: over 90 percent of the defendants were African-American men.

Gradually, Johnnie began to recognize the behavior of police officers in the black community and the often brutal sense of power they wielded at whim. In the inner circles of the LAPD, officers often joked about giving black men an "attitude test." If a suspect didn't answer questions to their liking or with the proper politeness, they would dispense "curbside justice"—a severe beating.

Another long-standing practice of the police department, which is still an issue today, was the pulling over of black or Latino motorists strictly because of their race, rather than for any suspicious behavior. The practice of viewing race an as indicator of criminal behavior is known as "racial profiling," although victims of this prejudicial treatment have nicknamed it "driving while black" (DWB). Even today, DWB is a widespread phenomenon. Some studies have shown that 72 percent of all routine traffic stops involve African-American drivers, despite the fact that blacks make up only about 15 percent of the driving population.

It is common for highway patrolmen to pull over black and Latino "suspects" for minor traffic violations that would usually be overlooked, such as failure to signal a lane change, following too closely behind another vehicle, or driving too slowly. Minority motorists are often stopped if they are driving an expensive vehicle. The idea is to find any reason to stop the vehicle so that it may be searched for drugs. Federal legislation to stop the practice of racial profiling was finally passed by Congress in 1998.

However, for Johnnie Cochran Jr. in the mid-1960s, there was no one fighting against these common patterns of police abuse. Cochran watched as officers took the stand and lied about defendants' behavior in order to justify police actions. What troubled him most was that as a lawyer for the prosecution, he was an accomplice of the police. The final straw came in a seemingly routine 148 case. A black man from South Central Los Angeles had been badly beaten by two officers from the LAPD's 77th Division. Johnnie remembered that both of the defendant's eardrums had been ruptured, the orbit of one of his eyes had been fractured, and he was bruised from head to toe. His account on the witness stand silenced the courtroom. Cochran watched him

Johnnie Cochran's first big case was the 1963 obscenity trial of comedian Lenny Bruce. Although he lost the case, Johnnie was making a name for himself as one of the city's best prosecutors.

from the prosecution table and knew he was telling the truth. When it was time for Johnnie to cross-examine the shaken man, Johnnie said, "No questions, Your Honor." The defendant was acquitted. Johnnie had seen enough. Later that day, he went to his superiors to inform them that he would no longer prosecute 148s.

Johnnie attempted to explain his inner conflict about his job to his wife, but Barbara had grown accustomed to the lifestyle afforded by her husband's $608-a-month job, and feared the uncertainty of their financial future if he left the department. Their toddler, Melodie, would also be affected if Johnnie wasn't able to survive in his own law practice. This would be the first major divide between Johnnie and Barbara; they were unaware that the rift would deepen over the years.

Disheartened and unfulfilled, Cochran left the city attorney's office in March 1965. He quickly joined another former deputy city attorney, Gerald D. Lenoir, and together they started a modest law firm. Lenoir was a small African-American man from New Orleans who kept Johnnie in stitches with his sense of humor. Ironically, most of their clients were charged with violating Section 148. These young black men would arrive at the office wrapped in bandages and peppered with bruises. From his experience in the city attorney's office, Cochran knew these cases against the police were virtually lost causes. He knew that judges and jurors would automatically decide in favor of any police officer who faced a black defendant, so Johnnie would offer his clients the chance to accept a deal, often a lesser plea of "no contest" to the charge of disturbing the peace. This was unfair to the defendants, yet Johnnie knew the alternative of more jail time would be worse. The African-American community in Los Angeles was also aware of the injustice in the legal system. Tension between the police and blacks was growing.

On August 13, 1965, Johnnie and Barbara were moving into a new home in the predominantly black, middle-class neighborhood of Leimert Park. That night, the discontent, anger, and frustration of Los Angeles' poor black communities erupted in a destructive act of rebellion and protest against the unfair treatment of blacks by the Los Angeles police. In the section of the city known as Watts, businesses were burned down, cars were overturned, and enraged black citizens filled the streets.

The incident that sparked the Watts riots had happened two days earlier. Two young black men, Marquette and Ronald Frye, had been stopped by the police for reckless driving. As they talked with the officers on the side of the road, they were joined by their mother. An argument between the Fryes and the police officers ensued, culminating in the arrest of Marquette and his mother. However, the commotion had attracted a crowd, and many people were angered by what they felt was police use of excessive force in arresting Mrs. Frye. Police reinforcements were called, agitating the growing crowd even more.

To get the crowds under control, the National Guard was summoned. LAPD Chief William Parker attempted to target the people who were encouraging the crowd to rebel. At a press conference about the riots, he stated that "necessary force would be used to restore order, to effect arrests and to protect officers from bodily harm." As a result, large groups of people were taken into custody on charges ranging from possession of stolen weapons and breaking and entering to felonious assault, theft, arson, and inciting to riot.

The Watts riots lasted for six days in a terrible outpouring of rage. More than 600 buildings were destroyed by looting and arson. The property loss totaled over $200 million. Horrifyingly, 35 people, mostly African Americans, lost their lives, and more than 1,000 people were injured.

As a result of the rioting, more than 4,000 adults and juveniles were arrested. A great number of those booked ended up in the law office of Lenoir and Cochran. So many potential clients called that August 1965 became Johnnie's most lucrative month since beginning his law career, with roughly $5,000 a day pouring in.

Yet Cochran could not escape the awful paradox surrounding his good fortune. The money came as a direct result of the biggest public protest of police injustice to date. It was in this context that Cochran would rethink his role as a defense attorney. As he watched Chief Parker announce the restoration of order, saying of the black rioters, "We've got them dancing like monkeys in a cage," Johnnie stewed in his own anger over the consistently uphill battle his clients endured to extract justice from an organization seemingly rotten to the core with racism. But, as Johnnie said to himself, "Burning of Watts, no matter how great the provocation—and it was great—could not advance that struggle."

After the riots, California governor Pat Brown formed a commission to study the causes. Headed by John McCone, the commission issued a report, entitled *Violence in the City*, that found the riots were a manifestation of much deeper and more prevalent issues: high jobless rates in the inner city, poor housing, bad schools, lack of health care, and a mistrust of the police. The McCone commission concluded that these problems were widespread, and the remedies costly and time consuming. The report recommended that the city make improvements in employment by developing job training programs; in education by providing preschool education and remedial education courses, and by decreasing class sizes; and in law enforcement community relations by establishing procedures enabling citizens to complain about police and by

increasing community relations efforts by local police precincts. However, many people felt that, despite these recommendations, the city of Los Angeles made no real effort to address the problems or to rebuild the neighborhoods that had been destroyed.

The Watts riots caused Johnnie to feel an overwhelming sense of duty to protect the constitutional rights of his clients. As the fires were beginning to smolder out around Los Angeles, the fire within Cochran to pursue justice for the disenfranchised of his community began to rage.

In the summer of 1965, a few months after Johnnie Cochran left his position as a city prosecutor because of inner conflict over police mistreatment of African Americans, rage at the LAPD and the justice system boiled over. The Watts Riots lasted for four days and resulted in over $200 million in property damage. More than 600 buildings were burned, including the ones pictured here.

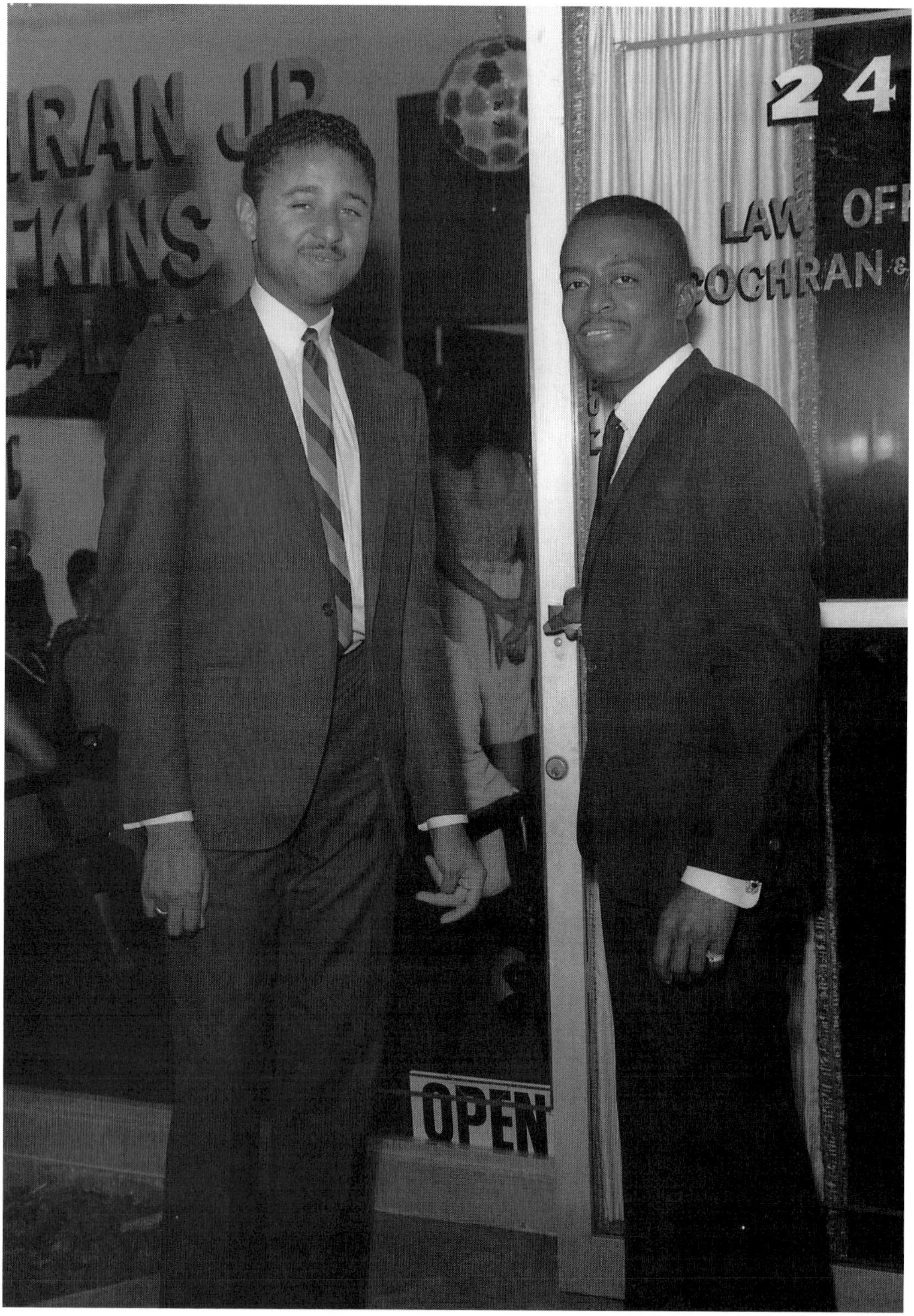
24
LAW
COCHRAN
OPEN

4

CHARGED WITH RESISTING
A POLICE OFFICER

───── ❧ ─────

I N THE WAKE of the 1965 Watts riots, Johnnie decided it was time to infuse his renewed energy for justice into his own private legal practice. He left his good friend Gerald Lenoir and opened a practice by himself. His office was located on Wilshire Boulevard—the mark of a lawyer who had arrived.

His office was modest, filled mostly with furniture from his own home. He hired a secretary who used a rented IBM typewriter. Most of Cochran's first clients had been referred to him by his father, but the office soon grew so busy that Johnnie had to hire a partner, Nelson L. Atkins, a former deputy city attorney whom Johnnie had known since high school.

One day in May 1966, Johnnie got a call from an old UCLA buddy, Herbert Avery, who was now a doctor at the Los Angeles County Medical Center. One of his patients, Barbara Deadwyler, was in serious need of legal help. Johnnie knew the name: her husband, Leonard Deadwyler, had recently been shot to death by an LAPD officer who had pulled him over for speeding.

Intrigued, Johnnie visited Barbara Deadwyler at the medical center. Between sobs, Barbara told Johnnie what had happened a few days earlier. Barbara was eight months pregnant, and she, Leonard, and a friend, Gamalyel Ferguson, were on their way to a store to buy baby clothes. As they drove, Barbara experienced what she thought were labor pains. Barbara's three previous children had been born prematurely, so labor pains a

Smiling Johnnie Cochran (right) and partner Nelson Atkins stand proudly in front of their new law office at 244 Wilshire Boulevard. The new firm of Cochran and Atkins would soon earn a reputation for defending the victims of police abuse.

43

month early were not necessarily a false alarm. She asked her husband to drive to the hospital immediately.

In rural Georgia, where the Deadwylers had lived before moving to Los Angeles, motorists in an emergency would tie a white handkerchief to their radio antenna. This signaled other drivers to move out of the way. It was also common for police officers to provide assistance when they saw the white handkerchief fluttering from the antenna. As the Deadwyler's car sped up Avalon Boulevard, toward the Los Angeles County Medical Center, LAPD squad cars pulled behind them, lights flashing. Believing his wife needed hospital care immediately, and perhaps recalling past police escorts of vehicles in emergency situations, Leonard continued driving. He finally stopped when an officer pulled alongside Leonard and aimed his gun inside the Deadwyler's car, ordering them to pull over. When the car was halted, police officer Jerold Bova approached the passenger side with his gun drawn. He leaned into Barbara's window, reaching toward the ignition key.

Later, Bova would claim that the Deadwyler's car suddenly moved forward. The sudden jerk generated a reflex action to grab his gun even tighter. It inadvertently discharged, firing a fatal bullet into Leonard Deadwyler's chest.

Police would later report that Leonard was very drunk, which had caused him to disobey the police officer's orders. The official autopsy seemed to support this claim. It found that Leonard's blood-alcohol concentration (BAC) was .35. This is a very high level; today, drivers can be prosecuted if their BAC is higher than .10, and a level of .40 or higher is often fatal.

However, many people were suspicious of the coroner's report. At the high BAC that the coroner claimed, Deadwyler would have been unable to speak coherently or drive. He might possibly have been unconscious. And both Barbara Deadwyler and Gamalyel Ferguson said that Leonard had not been intoxicated.

Cochran was moved as he stood over Barbara's

hospital bed listening to the pregnant woman recount the events of her husband's last moments. He wanted the truth about the Deadwyler shooting to come out, both to serve justice and to restore Leonard Deadwyler's reputation. Johnnie agreed to take the case.

Evelle J. Younger, the district attorney of Los Angeles, ordered a special hearing, called a coroner's inquest, to examine the facts surrounding Leonard's shooting. The coroner's inquest would determine if officer Bova had acted improperly. If so, the city could prosecute the policeman for the shooting. A hearing officer would preside over the inquest, and the case would be judged by a seven-person jury. A representative of the district attorney's office would question all of the witnesses. Normally, other attorneys did not participate in a coroner's inquest. However, Younger allowed Cochran to sit with the deputy district attorney in charge of the case,

Barbara Deadwyler, escorted by Los Angeles County sheriff deputies, attends the coroner's inquest into the shooting death of her husband, Leonard. Eight months pregnant and wearing a red-striped maternity dress, Deadwyler gave a two-hour account of the shooting that silenced the crowd of nearly 1,000 people at the hearing. Despite her compelling testimony, the jury decided LAPD officer Jerold Bova's shooting of Leonard Deadwyler was an accident, and the case was closed.

John Provenzano, and agreed that Provenzano would call the witnesses that Johnnie wanted to testify, and would ask them Cochran's questions.

More than 1,000 people attempted to crowd into Courtroom 12, where the inquest was being held in downtown Los Angeles. This trial marked the first time in history that deputies searched some of the people attending the proceedings. Television news cameras, photographers, and reporters from local papers were also packed inside, awaiting the truth about Leonard's shooting. His killing was yet another chapter in the city's growing saga of racially charged incidents involving the police department.

A hush descended upon the packed room as Barbara Deadwyler took the stand. With a steady voice, she recounted her story. The widow claimed she had not smelled alcohol on Leonard's breath that day. She told how her husband asked several people for the fastest route to the hospital after she complained of her pains. Provenzano asked if she saw any speed-limit signs, but Barbara responded that her pain had been so unbearable that she hadn't noticed. When Mrs. Deadwyler was asked about her husband's shooting, her composure suddenly crumbled. Barbara described the reaction of officer Bova after she asked him why her husband was shot.

"He didn't say anything," she told the courtroom. "He just put his gun back in his holster and turned around and walked to the back of the car."

After two hours of testifying, Barbara Deadwyler collapsed, exhausted. A deputy sheriff gave her some smelling salts to revive her, then assisted her from the witness stand.

Cochran's next witness, Gamalyel Ferguson, had been in the back seat of the car when Leonard Dead-wyler was shot. He testified that the car did not move after Deadwyler had parked, contrary to Bova's claim.

As the case made its way to the coroner's jury, Cochran believed he had established that officer Bova had been reckless and negligent, and that this caused

Deadwyler's death. However, the seven-member jury saw differently. In a split verdict, the jury found that while Leonard died "at the hands of another," Officer Bova's discharge of his revolver was accidental. This result convinced the district attorney to close the Deadwyler case for good.

Cochran was devastated. However, although he lost the case, the young lawyer was admired in the black community for his efforts and respected by his peers for the class with which he handled the verdict. Yet it was this verdict that would haunt Johnnie Cochran during future trials involving police misconduct. For Cochran, the Deadwyler case reinforced the importance of every American's basic human right to be treated fairly by the men and women sworn to protect and serve them, and the importance of seeking justice when that basic right has been violated.

The late 1960s were a time of many personal changes for Johnnie Cochran. His wife, Barbara, gave birth to their second daughter, Tiffany, in 1969. However, although they were united in their love for this new baby girl, their marriage was suffering. Heated arguments between Barbara and Johnnie would grow in frequency until both could no longer stand it. They decided to separate for a while.

It was during this long separation that Cochran met Patty Sikora, the secretary of his leasing agent. Sikora had initially sought Cochran's legal advice for her own divorce. Their marital problems brought the two together, and they began dating. However, despite the birth of their son, Jonathan, the relationship between Johnnie and Patty never gelled. The two eventually drifted apart, but Johnnie later said he was always a consistent and doting presence in Jonathan's life. He and Barbara got back together to try to patch things up, but their marital discord continued.

Professionally, Johnnie was entering another phase of his career. In late 1966, Cochran and Atkins added a third partner to the firm, Irwin Evans. They nicknamed

Johnnie Cochran with his first wife, Barbara, and daughters Melodie and Tiffany, at a party. Although Johnnie's professional life was very successful, his marriage to Barbara was troubled, and they divorced shortly after this photo was taken, in 1977.

him "Big Red," reflecting his height and decidedly auburn hair. Cochran would soon be embroiled in another important case involving the Los Angeles Police Department. This one pitted the LAPD against a militant activist group, the Black Panthers.

The Black Panther party was rooted in the Black Power movement of the 1960s. The men who advocated Black Power did not agree with the Reverend Martin Luther King's method of achieving racial equality through nonviolent protest. Instead, they promised violence in order to achieve the rights they deserved. As Stokely Carmichael, leader of the activist group Student Nonviolent Coordinating Committee (SNCC) and the man who coined the term "Black Power," explained, "I'm not going to beg the white man for anything I deserve. I'm going to take it."

Inspired by this philosophy, and sparked by the February 1965 assassination of civil rights leader Malcolm X, the Black Panther Party for Self-Defense emerged. The group's mission was to patrol African-American neighborhoods and monitor the treatment of blacks by police. The panther was chosen to symbolize the organization because a panther does not attack unprovoked, but when it is threatened it will retaliate viciously to defend itself. The Black Panthers ascribed to the revolutionary methods of men like Ernesto "Che" Guevara, who had been one of the main guerrilla leaders in Fidel Castro's successful 1959 revolution in Cuba. Guevara had then left to foster revolution in other Latin American countries.

In Oakland, California, the Black Panther Party was founded by Huey Newton, Bobby Seale, and David Hilliard. The Black Panthers believed they had witnessed unjustified, racially motivated police attacks of blacks in Oakland. The Panthers felt it was necessary to arm themselves and patrol the streets to protect African Americans from police abuse. For instance, if the Panthers witnessed the arrest of a black man or woman, they would remain on the scene to make sure that the police followed proper procedures. Black Panthers wore a standard uniform—leather jackets and black berets—and many openly carried guns; this, the Panthers felt, was for protection from police harassment.

While many white Americans had supported Martin Luther King's nonviolent Civil Rights movement, they feared Black Power and the Black Panthers' advocacy of violent revolution to achieve social change. In response to the growing number of armed Black Panthers, California governor Ronald Reagan generated legislation that prohibited citizens from carrying unconcealed weapons in public. The Panthers

The continued difficulty of the civil rights movement to gain equality for African Americans, and the assassinations of Malcom X (right) in 1964 and Dr. Martin Luther King (left) in 1968, led some angry blacks to form militant organizations like the Black Panther Party for Self-Defense. One of the goals of the Los Angeles Black Panthers was to protect members of the African-American community from what they perceived as a racist police force and justice system.

marched on the state capital, Sacramento, in 1967 to protest the measure. However, media coverage of this march cemented the image of the Black Panther Party as a group of gun-toting radicals advocating violence.

What was not as widely publicized was that the Black Panthers also developed social programs to serve the needs of the black community. The group expanded from its local base to become a national organization that supported activities such as the Free Breakfast for Children Program, the Free Food Program, the Free Testing for Sickle Cell Anemia Program, the Free Shoes and Clothing Program, the Free Bussing to Prisons Program, and the Legal Assistance Program. The Panthers also built education centers in poor

African-American communities.

Despite these community efforts, fear of Black Panther violence caused law-enforcement officials to label the group as dangerous. Local, state, and federal officers embarked on a campaign to destroy the organization. The FBI flooded the party with informants and federal agents who served as spies to relay information back to the Bureau on the Black Panthers' activities. By the end of 1969, several Black Panthers had been killed during confrontations with the police, and many others had been arrested for inciting riots and violence. In Los Angeles, there had been several shootouts between the Panthers and members of the LAPD's Criminal Conspiracy Division. These had added to the racial tension in the city.

Before sunrise on the morning of December 8, 1969, officers from the LAPD Criminal Conspiracy Division descended upon the Black Panthers' headquarters. They were dressed in black and armed with assault weapons. The department would later claim that the officers went to the Central Avenue headquarters to serve a misdemeanor warrant.

Melvin Smith, a member of the Black Panthers, was the first to notice the police. He promptly alerted the other members, who were fast asleep. Then Smith opened fire on the officers, who took cover and fired back. After a lengthy exchange of bullets, during which three officers and six Panthers were wounded, the Black Panthers surrendered. Thirteen members of the group were arrested. They were charged with over 70 offenses, the most serious being conspiracy to murder police officers.

Later, it was discovered that Melvin was an FBI informant. This may explain why he was the first to notice the encroaching officers, and why he was the first to shoot, inviting the police officers to return fire.

None of the defendants could afford legal representation. Their constitutional right to an attorney could not be met by the Los Angeles County Public Defender Office because of a conflict of interest: it was already representing Melvin Smith. Therefore, Superior Court Judge George Dell appointed his old friend, Johnnie Cochran Jr., to represent one of the Panthers, Willie Stafford, in what came to be known as the "LA Shootout" trial.

Cochran had mixed feelings about the Black Panthers. On one hand, he respected their serious commitment to social activism, but he also viewed some of the members as thugs who had joined the party because of its hip, gang-like appeal. In addition to Stafford, whom he believed fell into the latter category of Party members, Cochran would end up defending several of the 12 men on trial, including the leader of the Panther's Los Angeles office, Elmer "Geronimo" Pratt.

Pratt was a highly decorated Vietnam veteran, who had joined the Black Panthers shortly after returning from service in Southeast Asia. Because of his military background, the FBI had always regarded him with suspicion. Pratt had risen to an important position in the decision-making body of the entire Panther organization, and he was responsible for the Los Angeles division.

In the midst of the LA Shootout trial, Pratt's pregnant wife Sandra was found dead in a sleeping bag that had been tossed alongside a dirt road. She had been shot through the stomach, killing her and their unborn baby. At the time, the Black Panthers were split into two opposing factions: those who followed one of the party's founders, Huey Newton, and those who followed another member, Eldridge Cleaver, who was then living in a self-imposed exile in Algeria.

Pratt, a Cleaver supporter, believed members of the Newton faction were behind the murder of his wife. Members of both camps were defendants in the LA Shootout trial, and although free on bail, were present in court one morning before the members of the jury were let inside. Suddenly, the Cleaver faction began attacking the Newton supporters, throwing briefcases, chairs, and anything else close by that could be used as a weapon. A full-fledged court-room brawl erupted, which had to be quelled by deputies armed with shotguns. From that day forward, the defendants' arms and legs were chained in the courtroom.

But the trial continued without additional incident. As Cochran made his closing statement, he argued that the police had purposefully harassed the Panthers, hoping to provoke retaliation. He accused Melvin Smith of being an "Uncle Tom," who sold out others to foster a cozy relationship with the police. Cochran stressed the public's misconceptions about the Black Panthers, emphasizing their various social programs and community involvement. "If you find the defendants guilty," he concluded, "you are exonerating the police action and setting a precedent . . . that the doorways of the people in the ghetto can be kicked down at will."

The jury consisted of six African Americans, three Latinos, two whites, and an Asian American. Cochran knew this jury reflected the racial makeup of Los Angeles and was certain it would weigh the evidence fairly. On December 20, 1971, the jury acquitted the Black Panthers on all of the serious charges, including conspiracy to commit murder, although Stafford and Pratt were convicted of a lesser crime, conspiracy to possess contraband weapons.

This would not be the last time the paths of Cochran and Pratt would converge. Cochran couldn't know it at the time, but several months later Pratt would again seek him as defense counsel. Cochran had no way of knowing that this case would take over 25 years to resolve.

Johnnie Cochran successfully defended Elmer "Geronimo" Pratt and other Black Panthers involved in the LA Shootout case in 1969. A few months after Pratt was acquitted of the charges against him, he would seek out Cochran again to represent him in a murder case.

5

MR. DISTRICT ATTORNEY

B Y 1977 JOHNNIE Cochran was fully immersed in his private law practice. He had won the highest award given to a criminal lawyer in the city, the Los Angeles Criminal Courts Bar Association's Jerry Gersler award, and he was never at a loss for clients. Yet despite his tremendous good fortune, he had disappointments both personal and professional: the continuing difficulties in his marriage to Barbara, and the upsetting conviction of Geronimo Pratt for Susan Olsen's murder—a conviction Cochran felt was unsupported by the evidence against his client. Despite this frustrating loss, Johnnie Cochran continued fighting police misconduct, until he received a phone call that would alter the course of his career. On the other end of the phone was John Van de Kamp, the Los Angeles County district attorney. He told Johnnie that he had something important to discuss, and asked if they could meet. When they got together, at a swanky social club in downtown Los Angeles, Van de Kamp surprised Cochran by offering him the position of assistant district attorney.

For one of the rare times in his life, Johnnie Cochran Jr. was caught off-guard. He liked his successful private law practice and the freedom it offered. Also, the job would involve a severe pay cut—from $300,000 a year in private practice to the $49,000-a-year salary of a public official. However, if he accepted the assistant DA job, Cochran

Los Angeles district attorney John K. Van de Kamp announces the appointment of his new assistant district attorney, Johnnie L. Cochran Jr. As the number-three man in the DA's office, Cochran would try to change the system from within.

would be the number three man in the office, over-see the general administrative duties for all 600 prosecutors, and directly oversee the 85 deputy DAs assigned to the Juvenile Division, the Consumer and Environmental Protection divisions, the Sexual Crimes Unit, and the Special Investigations Division (SID). This last piece of information interested Cochran the most, because the SID investigates allegations of police and governmental misconduct. Cochran believed the legal system of Los Angeles to be corrupt to the core, from the police to the judges. He had spent much of his professional career working toward fighting police abuse and injustice; here was his chance to change the system from the inside.

Van de Kamp, Los Angeles mayor Tom Bradley, old friends, and even Cochran's father urged him to take the position. The sole voice of discontent was his wife, Barbara, who worried about the drop in salary. Despite her concerns, Cochran was convinced that he had to take advantage of the opportunity. He agreed to take the job.

This was the final straw for Barbara, who took their daughters, Melodie and Tiffany, and moved out of their home while Johnnie was at work. Cochran later wrote that he learned his wife was leaving when a neighbor called him at his office, wondering why a moving van was in front of the Cochran home. Johnnie returned to the house to find it had been emptied of all furniture, and their joint bank account had been depleted as well. By the end of the year, they were divorced.

In January 1978, Johnnie L. Cochran Jr. began serving his appointment as Los Angeles County's first African-American district attorney. He was working with a hot young prosecutor named Gil Garcetti, whom Van de Kamp had hired to head SID. As a team, Cochran and Garcetti were enthusi-astic about prosecuting police officers who abused

In 1977, Johnnie Cochran received the Los Angeles Criminal Courts Bar Association's Jerry Gersler award, the highest honor for an attorney practicing in the city.

their authority. However, despite Van de Kamp's desire to change the public's perception of the district attorney's office, Cochran and Garcetti's first experience in a widely publicized case indicated that it would be very difficult to reform the Los Angeles legal system.

On the morning of January 3, 1979, Eulia Love, a 39-year-old African-American homeowner, was visited by a Southern California Gas Company employee. He intended to shut off the gas to her home until her past-due bill, $22.09, was paid in full. Love, a recent widow, was at her home on Orchard Avenue with two of her three daughters. The family had been forced to survive on social security payments of $680 a month after the death of her husband in June 1978 from sickle-cell anemia. Money was tight, and the gas company had been to Love's home several times before to collect for past-due bills.

When serviceman John Ramirez arrived at the house, his repeated knocks were met with silence. When Ramirez walked to the side of the house where the gas was connected, Love came to the window and spoke with him. One witness, a neighbor, later described the verbal exchange as an argument. As Ramirez knelt to disconnect the gas, Love came out of the house, picked up a long-handled garden shovel, and approached him. According to his later testimony, she swung at him once and missed, then swung again, this time striking Ramirez on the arm. Ramirez ran back to his truck and left.

While the gas company employee was getting medical attention for his injury and telling the police what had happened, Love and her 12-year-old daughter, Tammy, walked to a local grocery store to purchase a money order for $22.09—the exact amount of money she owed the gas company. Meanwhile, the police instructed two other gas company employees to drive to Love's neighborhood, but ordered them not to do anything until patrolmen arrived.

Eulia and Tammy Love were on their way home with the money order, tucked safely inside Love's large shoulder purse, when they noticed two gas company vehicles, a truck and a car, parked on her street. Love approached the servicemen and asked if her gas would be turned off. One of the men told her that it would not, saying he was just there on a break. This serviceman later testified that Love had cursed at him, yelling that she would not pay an $80 bill, but she would pay the $20.

Later, investigators would understand her meaning. Love owed the Department of Water and Power more than $80, and she was $69 delinquent in payments to the gas company. The $22.09 was the minimum payment required to keep the gas service connected.

The man from the gas company said he saw her rummaging through her purse, but was unaware she had the money. Love's 15-year old daughter, Sheila, who was inside the house, later testified that Tammy came in and told her that their mother was trying to pay the servicemen, but that they rolled up their window and refused to accept her money. Love then walked back to her house, got an 11-inch kitchen knife, and walked out to her front lawn.

Two LAPD patrolmen, Edward Hopson, 43, and Lloyd O'Callaghan, 25, had been dispatched to handle the problem between Love and the gas company workers. Hopson, who was black, and O'Callaghan, who was white, arrived at Eulia Love's yellow stucco three-bedroom home to find her walking back and forth holding the knife. The officers exited their car, and Love approached them. The officers drew their guns and warned her to drop the knife.

It was at this point that the facts became clouded. Witnesses said that Love turned her back on the officers and began walking toward her house, still gripping the knife. Eulia Love's daughters walked out to the lawn to try to calm their mother down. Both later testified that O'Callaghan approached Love from behind, hit her on the shoulder to knock her down, then shot her on the ground. A neighbor said she saw O'Callaghan knock something from her hand, and then both Eulia and O'Callaghan fell to the ground. The neighbor testified that both bent over to pick something up, then Love stood up, raised the knife over her head, and was fired upon by the officers. One of the gas company servicemen said that Mrs. Love never stood up. He recalled that the first shot was fired while she was on her knees, bringing the knife upward.

These stories differed from the official report

provided to LAPD chief Daryl Gates. "Love abruptly rose to a standing position and simultaneously took one step rearward," the police department's internal investigators wrote. "She raised her right hand above her head and faced west toward officer O'Callaghan. She continued to hold the knife by the tip with the handle upward. The suspect slowly drew her right hand and arm rearward above her right shoulder, apparently preparatory to throwing . . . Officer O'Callaghan believed Love was about to throw the knife at him." The report went on to explain how Love "threw the knife at O'Callaghan after several rounds had been fired."

Witnesses said that first there was one shot, and then a barrage of 11 shots from the two officers. As the sound of gunfire faded away, Eulia Love lay dead on her front lawn, her daughters witnesses to their mother's shooting. The $22.09 money order was still in her purse.

Cochran and Garcetti believed the two policemen should be charged with manslaughter, especially after their own investigation found that O'Callaghan had a long history of treating African Americans brutally. However, Van de Kamp refused to prosecute the officers for the shooting. Cochran would later recall the moment this decision was made as "devastating."

Although Cochran's former law partners Nelson Atkins and Irwin Evans sued the city for Eulia Love's family, settling out of court for almost $1 million, Cochran realized that an overwhelming amount of evidence would be necessary for the DA's office to pursue cases of police misconduct. He and Garcetti were put off by a standard procedure in cases of police shootings. In the past, the district attorneys had relied solely on the reports of police inspectors. The prosecutors felt something had to be done to ensure that law-enforcement agencies were kept in check. Together, Garcetti and Cochran founded what became known as the Rollout Unit of the SID. A deputy district attorney and an investigator from

the DA's office would be required to inspect the scene of every police shooting within their jurisdiction. From that point forward, the police would not be relied upon to investigate their own potential misconduct.

Cochran also made significant changes within the Sexual Crimes Unit. Along with recruiting more female prosecutors, Cochran developed a system that eased the discomfort of rape victims as they attempted the difficult task of prosecuting their attackers. The victim's initial trauma would often be exacerbated by having to repeat her account of the rape over and over to different deputy district attorneys. Under

As a member of the district attorney's office, Johnnie Cochran created the "Rollout Unit" of the Special Investigations Division (SID). Under this new policy, whenever there was a shooting involving the Los Angeles Police Department, an investigator and deputy from the DA's office were required to inspect the scene and write a report. Cochran believed the police department was corrupt; the LAPD would no longer be allowed to perform its own investigations.

Johnnie Cochran was honored in 1979 by the Brotherhood Crusade as an African-American pioneer in the legal field, an honor he received again in 1994.

Cochran's new system, a single deputy DA would be in charge of a case from start to finish.

Cochran also founded the Los Angeles County Domestic Violence Council, and he changed the LAPD's method of handling domestic violence calls. Previously, police assessed the gravity of abuse by the amount of blood that had been spilled or the number or bruises and cuts on the victim, and made a judgment call. If the victim didn't appear too bloody or badly injured, the officers would view the situation as a family dispute and promptly leave to respond to more important calls. However, abuse isn't always obvious, and Cochran helped to institute a policy requiring officers to inform battered women that they were entitled to protection and assistance, and to provide a list of shelters and agencies assisting battered women.

Cochran's accomplishments in the district attorney's office were noticed by the California Trial Lawyers Association, which awarded him its 1979 Law Enforcement Officer of the Year for his "outstanding courageous and progressive leadership and for his fair administration of justice as assistant district attorney." That same year, Cochran was honored by the Brotherhood Crusade as an African-American pioneer in the legal field.

Although he worked to protect the rights of the African-American community in Los Angeles, Cochran was not afraid to speak out against the problems that he saw within that community. In 1979, LAPD officer Bernard Parks—who in 1997 would be elected chief of police—invited him to address the National Organization of Black Law Enforcement (NOBLE). NOBLE, based in Alexandria, Virginia, offers criminal justice–related training in the areas of promotional process and assessment center preparation, family violence, hate crimes, cultural diversity, equal employment opportunities, community partnerships, and community policing. NOBLE has an important and active role in policy making and development of law enforcement standards nationwide.

Cochran jumped at the chance to speak directly to the African-American contingent of the force. He wasn't sure what his topic should be, but he knew this would be a stellar opportunity to effect change "from the inside."

The issue of crimes committed by blacks against other African Americans was a hot topic during the late 70s. *Ebony* magazine had pushed it to the forefront with a report on the ways that black-on-black crime affected urban African Americans. Cochran thought an audience of black law enforcement officers was the perfect place to speak out about the issue. However, many of his friends advised against

In addition to being a respected attorney, Johnnie Cochran is also a powerful and popular public speaker. In the late 1970s, he gained a great deal of attention for his speeches about the problem of black-on-black crime.

the topic, believing his words would be taken out of context and used by white racists to show that a black deputy district attorney was denouncing his own race by speaking out against its criminal element. Some of Cochran's friends also thought he might be labeled an "Uncle Tom" by other blacks for aiding the establishment in speaking out against black crime.

Uncertain, Cochran asked his father for advice. Johnnie Sr. didn't buy any of Johnnie's friends' arguments, and urged him to speak out. "You can do what needs to be done because nobody expects it of you," Johnnie Sr. told his son. "Besides, it's the right thing to do."

That was all his son needed to hear. Cochran spoke candidly to the NOBLE audience, warning that the problem of black-on-black crime was approaching crisis proportions and could not be tolerated. "As African Americans active in the criminal justice system, we have a special responsibility to act in this matter since our community is suffering the most," he told the enthralled group of lawmen.

The speech was a success. The response among the members of NOBLE at the meeting and elsewhere was overwhelmingly positive. In the wake of the speech, a new dialogue was launched in Los Angeles between black law enforcement officers and black prosecutors in the offices of the DA and city attorney. Out of that discussion and pooling of information about crime within the black community came the district attorney's new Hardcore Gang Unit.

In 1980 Cochran made another highly regarded speech. This one, also about black-on-black crime, was delivered at the mid-year conference of the National Bar Association, held near San Francisco. This time, he denounced black crime apologists, who used excuses like racism and socioeconomic issues to justify the high level of black-on-black crime. In his speech, Cochran suggested firearms control and a community-wide effort to pitch in and deal with the problem head-on.

Despite the accolades he received for his bravery in speaking out, Cochran was still frustrated with the bureaucracy in the district attorney's office when he tried to pursue cases of police misconduct. Tensions between Cochran and Van de Kamp came to a head in 1980, when Cochran made another effort to free Geronimo Pratt, the Black Panther in whose innocence Cochran still steadfastly believed. Cochran wrote a personal letter to the Department of Corrections, once again advocating his client's innocence and asking for a new trial.

It was no secret how Cochran felt about Geronimo Pratt. Yet when Van de Kamp found out about Cochran's letter, he was infuriated. The DA's position had always been that Pratt was guilty of murdering the Santa Monica schoolteacher, and that his trial had been fair and by the book. Even though Cochran's letter had been written on his personal stationary, not the district attorney's letterhead, Van de Kamp was angry that Cochran had taken a public stance against the DA's position.

This incident would cause Cochran to have second thoughts about his ability to effect change within the system as an assistant DA. The brick wall of bureaucracy he once believed he could start chipping away from the inside just wouldn't give. He had already been disheartened by an incident with the Los Angeles Police Department that involved him directly.

While driving his seven-year-old son Jonathan and ten-year-old daughter Tiffany to buy toys, Cochran was pulled over by the police. Four squad cars surrounded Cochran's brown Rolls Royce, and officers approached their vehicle, aiming their guns at all three occupants. Cochran immediately felt the terror Leonard Deadwyler must have felt. The officers ordered Cochran to exit the car with his hands up and move to the curb. Fearing another Deadwyler situation, Cochran suppressed his anger and did exactly as he was told. One of the officers spotted Cochran's identification sitting on the driver's seat. When he flipped through the wallet, he found Cochran's gold district attorney badge. The policemen apologized, and an apology even came from LAPD chief Daryl Gates. But all the apologies in the world couldn't erase the utter humiliation and fear he and his two children had endured that day.

At the end of his three-year term in the district attorney's office, Cochran decided to return to private practice. In that capacity, his decisions would not be monitored, questioned, or hindered by someone higher in the administration. He would be free to pursue the kind of cases he wanted, free to be a voice for the voiceless in need of justice.

6

FIGHTING FOR JUSTICE

❧

O N JANUARY 2, 1981, armed with a renewed sense of purpose, Cochran headed for his first day at his new private practice. In his autobiography *Journey to Justice*, Cochran explained that he hoped to combine the idealism of Thurgood Marshall, the first African American to be appointed to the U.S. Supreme Court, with the stylish savvy of Leo Branton, a high-priced defense attorney he admired. Just five months later, an important case would come his way, offering him a chance to display both traits.

Ron Settles was a star running back for California State University at Long Beach. He had just finished his junior year, and hoped after graduation to be selected in the NFL draft. On June 2, 1981, the 21-year-old was driving his Triumph TR-7 sports car to a nearby junior high school, where he was employed as a part-time student teacher and coach. Settles was running late, and he decided to take a shortcut through the community of Signal Hill, an area south of Los Angeles and north of the port city of Long Beach. Signal Hill was notorious for its brutal police force.

Speeding through Signal Hill, Settles was stopped by police officer Jerry Lee Brown because he was driving 47 mph in an 25 mph zone. According to the official police account, Settles became "loud and obnoxious," forcing Officer Brown to call for backup.

Johnnie Cochran with his daughter, Tiffany, and second wife, Dale Mason. In the 1980s, after leaving the Los Angeles district attorney's office, both his personal and professional lives took off.

When the backup arrived, Settles allegedly pulled a nine-inch stainless steel knife from under his seat. The officers drew their guns and Settles promptly surrendered. When the police searched the car, they found a vial containing traces of cocaine and other drug paraphernalia. Settles was arrested for possession of cocaine, failing to produce an identification card, resisting arrest, and assaulting a police officer. What happened to Settles in a holding cell, after he was handcuffed and taken to the Signal Hill police station, would once again involve Johnnie Cochran in a case addressing police brutality.

Police said that once at the station, Settles made a phone call to his mother, who promptly arranged to bail him out. But before the bail was posted, at 2:35 P.M. police found Settles dead. He apparently had hung himself, using the mattress cover of the cell's bunk bed.

Days later, Ron Settles's parents, Donell and Helen Settles, showed up in Cochran's Century City office. They were convinced that Ron, their only child, was not the kind of person who would take his own life, and they begged Cochran to help them find out what really happened in their son's holding cell.

Johnnie didn't see any way this case could give the grieving parents the peace of mind they were seeking. The only witnesses to the discovery of Ron Settles's body were police officers; Cochran assumed that if misconduct had occurred, the other officers would lie to protect their guilty comrades. Also, Donell and Helen Settles were a working-class couple in their mid-forties, and they couldn't afford Cochran's regular attorney fees.

But the profound grief on the faces of Mr. and Mrs. Settles sitting in his office that day clutching a framed picture of their son, and his sympathy for a mother and father simply in search of the truth, moved Cochran to take the case.

To help prepare, Cochran sought the help of

attorney Mike Mitchell, a young lawyer he had met while serving as assistant district attorney. Mitchell was a graduate of the Harvard Law School and had served as an attorney for the Securities and Exchange Commission before beginning to practice as a civil-rights attorney. At the time, Mitchell was among a group of Los Angeles lawyers fighting against police abuse.

A coroner's inquest into the death of Ron Settles began two months later. Unlike the coroner's inquest in the Deadwyler case, Cochran and his legal team would now be allowed to call and question witnesses and to argue directly to the nine-person jury. This was a change that Cochran had pushed for after the Deadwyler case.

Because Ron Settles was a well-known athlete, the media covered the inquest intensively. Investigative reporters from local papers began to uncover a long history of brutality within the Signal Hill Police Department.

During the 11-day inquest, another man who was being held in the jail when Settles was booked testified that he had been taken out of the jail by authorities after hearing police officers beat Ron Settles, and before Ron's body was discovered. He also testified that the bed in Settles's cell did not have a mattress cover, even though police said their prisoner had used one to hang himself. When the Signal Hill police chief took the stand, he could not explain why all tape recordings of the radio traffic involving Ron's arrest had been mysteriously erased, or why his officers waited at least six minutes to call the paramedics after allegedly finding Settles hanging in his cell.

After five hours of deliberation, the jury at the inquest found that Ron Settles had "died at the hands of another and by other than accident." This prompted Cochran and Mitchell to file, on behalf of Donell and Helen Settles, a $50 million lawsuit against the city of Signal Hill for the wrongful death of Ron Settles.

Cochran was facing a self-protective police system, and he knew the fight would be uphill all the way. But he was stunned when his former boss, District Attorney John Van de Kamp, and former coworker, Gil Garcetti, decided to close the Settles case even though their investigation had uncovered a widespread pattern of misconduct in the Signal Hill police department. In a press conference announcing the closing of the case, Van de Kamp said, "There is insufficient evidence to establish the identity of anyone as the perpetrator of any crime directly related to Mr. Settles' death."

Cochran was frustrated that criminal charges would not be filed against those responsible for Settles's death. But Ron Settles's parents only wanted the truth about their son's death to come out. Cochran telephoned Donell and Helen Settles to ask that Ron's body be exhumed, so that it could be reexamined by medical experts. After Cochran was given the okay, two of the country's best pathologists, Michael Baden and Sidney Weinberg, examined the body in New York. They took X rays, and found that Ron had broken bones and bruises on his face, neck, and chest. These injuries had not been included in the original autopsy report conducted by the Los Angeles coroner's office; the staff had unquestioningly accepted the word of Signal Hill police who said that Settles had hanged himself.

As they examined the body, the two pathologists determined what they believed actually happened to Ron Settles. They found that he had suffered esophageal hemorrhaging. The injury, they felt, could only be caused by an outside force crushing the windpipe into the spine from one direction. Ron Settles had not hung himself, they concluded. He was choked to death, probably by a police carotid choke hold.

This particular hold was commonly used by the LAPD and other law-enforcement agencies to subdue

violent suspects. The officer would stand behind the suspect and wrap his baton around the front of the suspect's neck, pinching the carotid artery that runs between the middle of the collar bone and jaw line. When done correctly, the hold should cause unconsciousness in 10 to 20 seconds. When done incorrectly, however, it can be fatal.

The Los Angeles Police Department's training manual outlined in detail several types of choke holds. But the police training manual also stressed that the holds were to be applied only if verbal persuasion had failed to control the combative suspect,

After the death of Ron Settles, Johnnie Cochran was disappointed when Gil Garcetti, his former deputy at the DA's office, announced that the case would not be pursued.

and warned that the application of pressure in these holds must be stopped as soon as the suspect ceases to resist. In the case of Ron Settles, whose lifeless body lay on a coroner's table in New York, it was quite apparent that someone had applied a choke hold far beyond the stopping point.

Although the medical evidence pointed to the guilt of Signal Hill policemen, Gil Garcetti refused to reopen the criminal investigation. The civil lawsuit that Cochran had filed against Signal Hill was proceeding, but the stress of the ordeal was taking its toll on Helen Settles. She had a medical condition that had worsened after Ron's death. To avoid a long and painful trial that might cause her health to slip even further, Donell Settles asked Cochran to settle the case out of court as quickly as possible. Their attorney was disappointed, because he felt they had the evidence on their side, but he was also concerned with Helen's health. Cochran agreed to a $760,000 payment for Ron Settles's parents. At the time, this was among the largest settlements ever involving police misconduct in the state of California.

In the wake of the settlement, the Signal Hill police chief was fired, three council members were voted out, and a group of outside consultants was hired to reform the police department. Yet the most important result of the Settles case may have been the national attention it focused on police corruption and police use of the choke hold.

Soon after the Settles case, Cochran received a call from his old friend Herbert Avery, the physician who had referred Barbara Deadwyler to Cochran in 1966. Now Avery was seeking Cochran's legal services himself. He wished to sue the City of Los Angeles and two Los Angeles police officers because of an incident that had occurred six years earlier.

On July 25, 1976, Avery had been driving by his Los Feliz home when he spotted his son's car pulled over to the side of the road. His son and a friend

When noted forensic pathologist Michael Baden examined Ron Settles's body, he found that the deceased football player's windpipe had been crushed. The fatal damage had probably been caused by a carotid artery choke hold, he testified.

were being questioned by police. Avery approached the officers, identifying himself and telling the policemen that the car his son was driving belonged to him. According to Avery's account, one of the officers struck him in the chest with his baton and ordered him to leave the area. When the surgeon told the police officer that he lived there, the angry policeman pushed him off the sidewalk and choked him with a bar arm control hold.

The experience left Herb Avery in severe neck pain for the next six years. His ability to perform surgeries suffered as a consequence. Cochran smelled another chance to fight police misconduct. On behalf of Herb Avery, he sued the city and officers Larry

R. Goebel and Robert Sherman. A trial was set for December 1982.

In the long Superior Court trial, Cochran argued that Avery was attacked without provocation by the officers when he stopped on the Hollywood street to see why his son was being searched. Cochran also pointed out other unreasonable conduct of the two officers that preceded the application of the choke hold. The officers allegedly struck Avery with a fist, beat him with the baton, and kicked him in the legs. Deputy City Attorney Richards James countered by saying that Avery had provoked the attack by his belligerence and his refusal to cease interfering with routine police action. James also claimed that Avery had not been subdued by the bar arm during the confrontation.

The jury found Cochran's argument more convincing and awarded Herbert Avery $1.3 million. This was Cochran's first million-dollar verdict, although the judge would eventually reduce the amount of the award to $750,000. More important to Johnnie Cochran Jr., however, was the effect the verdict would have on his next case, which would lead the LAPD to eliminate the choke hold forever.

On March 27, 1982, James Thomas Mincey Jr., a 20-year-old African-American man, had been stopped and ticketed for speeding by two LAPD officers. They also cited him for a cracked windshield before sending him on his way. En route to his mother's house, two more police officers motioned him to pull over a few minutes later. This time, Mincey continued to drive. Several more patrol cars joined the pursuit, until Mincey stopped at his mother's house. When Mincey exited the car, police officers slammed him against the vehicle, sprayed him with liquid tear gas, handcuffed him, and threw him to the ground. An officer then allegedly applied a carotid choke hold to Mincey as his mother stood by, helplessly shouting for them to stop. The officer continued until Mincey stopped moving, then placed his motionless body in the back of the squad car. James Thomas Mincey died two weeks later without ever regaining consciousness.

Cochran filed a federal lawsuit on behalf of Mincey and his mother, Rozella Fowler, for $62 million in damages. The case never went to trial, because the city agreed to an undisclosed seven-figure out-of-court settlement. More importantly, representatives of the National Association for the Advancement of Colored People (NAACP), the Urban League, and the American Civil Liberties Union joined Cochran and Mike Mitchell in demanding that the police commission ban the use of the choke hold. Cochran argued that training at the L.A. Police Academy in the use of the choke hold was flawed. After deliberation, and against the recommendation of LAPD chief Daryl Gates, the city's police commission declared a moratorium on use of the choke hold unless the situation was "clearly life-threatening."

Cochran's professional career continued to flourish, and his life outside of the office was good as well. In 1981, Los Angeles mayor Tom Bradley, a fraternity brother of Cochran's at UCLA, asked him to become director of the commission that ran the city-owned Los Angeles International Airport, known as LAX. Bradley told Cochran that as airport commissioner he would set policy and see it through to completion. Bradley also needed someone capable of overseeing the sizable expansion of the airport's capacity to handle the heavy traffic expected for the upcoming 1984 Olympics. He was confident his friend Johnnie Cochran Jr. could handle the responsibility.

Cochran accepted the challenge, eventually serving three terms as director, from 1981 through 1993. His proudest moment was opening a new $124 million terminal for international flights, named for Tom Bradley, that made LAX the largest

Los Angeles mayor Tom Bradley at a 1983 press conference to unveil the new international terminal of the Los Angeles Airport. Bradley had appointed his friend Johnnie Cochran Jr. to head the airport authority and raise funds for the new terminal two years earlier.

international airport in the United States.

Cochran was flying high personally as well. While in Portland on airport authority business in 1982, Johnnie had been invited to a party held by a company that wanted to do business with LAX. At the event, he immediately noticed a woman named Dale Mason in the crowded room. As fate would have it, the only empty seat in the room was next to Johnnie. They engaged in conversation, and Cochran learned that Dale was the vice president of market-ing for the Atlanta-based company Gourmet Services, which was hosting the party. Cochran was immediately attracted to Dale's beauty, her focus and drive, and most important, her seemingly effortless ability to be both "charmingly cultivated and disconcertingly plainspoken," as Johnnie wrote in his autobiography.

They decided to extend the evening even further by sharing some ice cream. As they parted later that night, the two agreed to meet the following day for lunch, then later that evening for her boss's birthday celebration.

Over the next three years, Dale and Johnnie continued to date. He flew to her New Orleans hometown to meet her family, and Dale met Johnnie's children Melodie, Tiffany, and Jonathan. On March 1, 1985, Dale and Johnnie were married at the Bel Air Hotel in Los Angeles. The two spent a romantic honeymoon in Acapulco, Mexico, and in Europe. Johnnie felt that he had finally found a soulmate. With Dale's unwavering personal support, Johnnie felt unstoppable.

However, things were not always good for Johnnie Cochran. Returning from a social engagement one night in 1991, he and Dale received bad news about Johnnie's mother. Her health was bad, and she had been hospitalized. The next morning, Dale, Johnnie, his brother and sisters, his children, his ex-wife Barbara and Jonathan's mother Patty, all gathered at Hattie Cochran's bedside and prayed for her comfort. Johnnie Cochran Sr. sat silently at the foot of her bed as a weakened Hattie continued to speak with everyone in the room. She ordered Johnnie to take his father home to get some sleep, assuring him that they could return later that evening to spend time with her. When the family members left, Dale and Johnnie took Johnnie Sr. home and both father and son, mentally and physically exhausted, fell asleep.

In *Journey to Justice*, Johnnie recalled that when he awoke, he knew that his mother had died during his slumber. He was correct. Johnnie Sr. and his son joined the rest of their family at the hospital to say goodbye to the strong woman who had instilled in her son a firm reverence of God and the inner strength to pursue the goals located in the far reaches of his imagination.

Johnnie Cochran continued fighting against police misconduct. In 1992, he secured another landmark decision against the LAPD in a case involving Patty Diaz, a 13-year old Latino girl who was sexually assaulted by a police officer.

According to Cochran's own account, in January 1989, LAPD officer Stanley Tanabe, in full uniform, arrived at Patty's family's home at 3 A.M. He said he was there to check out a report of a woman screaming. Patty was asleep in a back bedroom when the officer walked into the room. While her 10-year old brother and 2-year old sister watched, Tanabe molested Patty in her bedroom. He then left the apartment, only to return five minutes later with a drawing of a suspect he said was being investigated. Again, Tanabe attempted to molest Patty.

The next day, Patty and her mother reported the incident to the police. Patty provided a description of the officer to a sergeant in the Hollywood Division, and said that she had previously seen Tanabe in the neighborhood driving a police car. However, the city did not make any attempt to investigate these allegations. The sergeant's log of Patty's complaint contained a thorough description of Tanabe, but was never given to the detectives who were assigned to investigate the case.

Thirty days later, Tanabe returned in full uniform to Patty's house, again claiming to be conducting an investigation. He attempted to molest Patty again, but this time the girl was able to escape to a neighbor's apartment and call the police. When the police arrived at the Diaz apartment, Tanabe was arrested. However, he was not held for the alleged crime. Instead, he was released on his own recognizance.

When this case reached Cochran's desk, he saw another opportunity to expose corruption within the Los Angeles Police Department. He sued the city for police misconduct. Cochran argued that Tanabe had violated Patty's civil rights by committing sexual battery while he was on duty. The attorney also claimed that the city had a history of failing to supervise its officers and to properly investigate citizen complaints against the police department. The wily lawyer brought up Tanabe's past, showing that before he was hired by the Los Angeles Police Department, he had been rejected for jobs with other police departments because tests showed psychological problems.

On August 6, 1992, the jury in the civil lawsuit awarded Patty and her mother $9.4 million dollars—the largest fine ever imposed against the city of Los Angeles in a civil rights case.

7

ATTORNEY TO THE STARS

By THE EARLY 1990s, Cochran was one of the country's best-known attorneys. Private investigator Clifford Mosby told *The American Lawyer*, "There's a widespread feeling that if you've suffered an injustice, he's the guy you want on your team." Everyone from panhandlers to celebrities knew of Cochran's ability to win lawsuits and criminal defense cases.

Cochran's private practice grew to include criminal defense and police brutality cases, insurance defense, entertainment and sports law, and securities work. His celebrity clients included Lou Rawls, Chaka Khan, Aretha Franklin, Stevie Wonder, George Clinton, and former Cleveland Browns running back-turned-actor/activist Jim Brown, whom Cochran successfully defended when Brown was accused of assaulting a 33-year-old schoolteacher.

In 1989, Cochran defended actor Todd Bridges against charges of attempted murder in the near-fatal shooting of an Los Angeles drug dealer at a crack house. Bridges was a child television star who had played Willis on the popular NBC sitcom *Diff'rent Strokes*. After the show was canceled in 1986, Bridges sank into a deep depression and a major drug habit, eventually getting into serious trouble with the law. With Cochran's legal guidance, Bridges was acquitted of charges of attempted involuntary manslaughter and assault with a deadly weapon.

Johnnie Cochran Jr., with wife Dale, had become one of the best-known attorneys in the country by the 1990s.

Michael Jackson, accused of sexually molesting a teenage boy, proclaims his innocence during a televised statement. The statement, suggested by Johnnie Cochran, was broadcast nationally on December 22, 1993. The lawsuit against Jackson was settled before it went to trial.

But Todd Bridges was far less well known than Cochran's next big celebrity client. In September 1993, pop superstar Michael Jackson was accused of sexually molesting a 13-year-old boy at the singer's Neverland Ranch in Santa Barbara, California.

Michael Jackson had probably been the most popular entertainer in the world during the previous decade. This made him a popular subject for the tabloid news media, which reported, often inaccurately, intimate details about his private life. As a result, Jackson was shy and reclusive. The accusation of sexual molestation opened his life up to public scrutiny by mainstream news organizations, as well as continued attacks by the tabloids. By November 1993, the relentless media coverage of the 13-year old boy's allegations led

Jackson to cancel a concert tour and seek refuge in Europe. At this time, Jackson's close friend, actress Elizabeth Taylor, contacted Johnnie Cochran, asking him to join the pop singer's legal team.

Cochran agreed to retain Jackson as a client. His first order of business was to convince Jackson to fly back to the United States and face the allegations head-on. Cochran advised the entertainer to proclaim his innocence in a live press conference. On December 22, Jackson gave a four-minute speech that was broadcast live on CNN, Court TV, MTV, E! Entertainment Television, and other networks. In it, the singer denied the accusation that had been brought against him.

While the world stirred in excitement over Jackson's message, Cochran set out to prevent the case from ever going to trial by attempting to reach an out-of-court agreement. By January 1994, Cochran was having regular meetings with Larry Feldman, the lawyer for Jackson's 13-year-old accuser. Feldman and Cochran were friends and had known each other for over 20 years. In an article in *The American Lawyer*, Feldman later said, "I never spoke to anyone on their side until [Cochran] came on board. It had been a bloody war every single day. But Johnnie and I had a mutual respect, and that certainly helped us in getting a resolution."

By mid-January, both sides had agreed to a settlement. Jackson agreed to pay an undisclosed amount of money to the boy. Part would be paid immediately; the remainder was placed in a trust fund. In return, the teen would not testify in any criminal investigations against Jackson. The settlement made it possible for Michael to avoid giving a deposition that was scheduled for January 18. There the singer, who took great pains to protect his privacy, would have had to discuss the most intimate aspects of his life. After the deposition was released, his private life would certainly have been exposed on the front pages of every newspaper around the world. Although some people viewed Jackson's unwillingness to go to trial and the court settlement as proof of the entertainer's guilt, Cochran and his legal team saw the agreement as a victory for Michael in keeping his good name. With the settlement, Jackson could continue to maintain his innocence. But the agreement also prohibited Michael from ever accusing the boy's family of attempting to extort money from Jackson.

While Cochran was in the midst of helping Michael Jackson, he was also actively suing the city of Los Angeles on behalf of Reginald Denny, Takao Hirata, Fidel Lopez, and Wanda Harris, all victims of a 1992 riot in South Central Los Angeles. The violence had been sparked by the acquittal of four white police officers accused of violating the civil rights of an African-American motorist, Rodney King.

On the night of March 3, 1991, King was chased at high speed by police. When his small white Hyundai was finally stopped, King allegedly hesitated when the police ordered him to get out of the car. Police said King then appeared to lunge at them. In response, an officer fired a 50,000-volt taser electric dart at the black motorist. The officers claimed King still refused to obey the instructions to lie flat on the ground. During the next two minutes, four police officers kicked Rodney King six times and struck him with 56 baton blows as 11 other LAPD officers stood by and watched.

Unbeknownst to the officers at the scene, a private citizen was videotaping the incident from his apartment balcony nearby. George Holliday, a plumbing store manager, was testing out his brand new video camera when he noticed the activity outside his window. He recorded the vicious beating.

Eighty-one seconds later, the incident appeared to be over and Holliday stopped the tape. He was unsettled by what he had just witnessed, and felt that this police behavior was newsworthy. Holliday contacted a local television news station, and sold them the tape for $500. The station then sold a copy to CNN for $100. On March 4, 1991, the entire world saw the violent beating of Rodney King.

The vivid depiction of Rodney King's beating at the hands of these LAPD officers was drastically different from what the officers had reported. The video showed a defenseless King writhing on the ground while being kicked and struck with batons. As a result of the beating, Rodney King suffered a shattered eye socket and cheekbone, broken legs, a concussion, and partial paralysis in his face. Four policemen—Officer Lawrence M. Powell, Probationary Officer Timothy Wind, Officer Theodore Briseno, and Sgt. Stacy C. Koon—were charged with assaulting King and with the use of excessive force.

Because of the videotape, and the extent of King's injuries, most people thought this particular incident of police brutality would be punished. However, attorneys for the four officers successfully argued that the trial be moved to the predominantly white suburb of Simi Valley because a fair trial in Los Angeles would be impossible given the amount of publicity. On April 29, 1992, the jury of eleven whites and one Filipino found the officers not guilty of assault with a deadly weapon, and acquitted three of the four officers of excessive use of force. The panel of six men and six women deadlocked on whether the remaining officer was guilty. Jurors believed the defense's justification for the beating that Rodney King was difficult to subdue and continually refused to follow police instructions. Jurors discounted the testimony of a California highway patrol officer who testified that she had tried to stop the beating and had noted the badge numbers of the officers involved to report them to authorities. The jurors also discounted the testimony of defendant Theodore Briseno, who said that his codefendants were "out of control" that night. Holliday's video was studied frame by frame, yet for some reason the jury did not find the beating as excessive as most of the country did.

The acquittal sparked a frustrated response in African-American communities. Disgruntled crowds began to gather in the streets of South Central Los Angeles as the social and racial implications of the verdict began to sink in. In effect, the jury's decision made it justifiable for police to brutally beat an already subdued suspect.

More and more people began to fill the streets, shouting about injustice. The intersection of Florence and Normandy streets became particularly volatile, as bottles were thrown against buildings, stores were looted, and fires were set. Angry rioters pelted passing automobiles with bottles, and drivers were pulled out onto the ground. In the midst of the riot, truck driver Reginald Denny attempted to maneuver his 18-wheeler through the intersection. He was stopped by angry rioters and pulled from his truck. Four black men proceeded to brutally beat Denny as news cameras captured the incident from helicopters hovering above the scene. One of Denny's assailants was seen throwing a brick at Denny, then kicking him before dancing over his unconscious body.

The attack on Reginald Denny was broadcast live on television for several minutes, yet no police appeared to intervene on Denny's behalf. In fact, television coverage showed repeated scenes of stores being looted as police stood in the background with orders not to intervene.

Johnnie Cochran first met with Reginald Denny while he was recuperating at the Santa Clarita home of his brother-in-law, Rick Montez. In the months following the beating, Denny had been approached by dozens of lawyers, all offering their services. But Montez's father-in-law belonged to a motorcycle club with Dominick Rubalcava, a lawyer who knew Johnnie Cochran. Rubalcava told him Johnnie that could help prevent anyone from taking advantage of Denny in his vulnerable state.

In the summer of 1993, Cochran filed a civil rights lawsuit in U.S. District Court for the Central District of California, claiming that the Los Angeles Police Department discriminated in its decision to withdraw its forces from the intersection of Florence and Normandy during the beginning stages of the riots while continuing to protect other areas. Due to that lack of police protection, which Cochran felt was rooted in racism, Denny, Hirata, and Lopez were injured and Harris' son was killed. Chief

Judge William Matthew Byrne Jr. eventually dismissed the suit, explaining that because Denny was white, the "equal protection" argument in Cochran's case was baseless. However, it was dismissed without prejudice, which meant that a modified lawsuit could be refiled. Cochran immediately refiled the complaint, including additional facts and legal arguments to support his equal protection claims. On January 31, 1994, Judge Byrne ruled that the lawsuit could continue, citing a 1989 Sixth Circuit ruling allowing white residents of Canton, Ohio, to claim that police had failed to protect them because they lived in a primarily black area. The Denny case was a victory for Cochran, and it was also a symbolic breakthrough. For the first time, a black person was defending a white person's civil rights in pursuit of justice against police oppression.

Cochran was developing a reputation as attorney to the stars, and his personal style went hand-in-hand

Cochran with truck driver Reginald Denny, who had been badly beaten during riots that broke out after the acquittal of four police officers in the Rodney King trial.

Rapper Snoop Doggy Dogg was represented by Cochran during his 1995 trial for murder.

with the famous people he represented. He drove to court in his Rolls Royce, with personalized plates reading "JC JR." He dressed in crisp, expensive suits, usually accented by a wildly bright tie from his extensive collection. His impeccable fashion taste, mixed with his unflappable demeanor in the courtroom, led colleagues to call him "flashy," or "silky smooth."

Another high-profile case followed the Reginald Denny litigation. Cochran was hired to defend rap star Snoop Doggy Dogg, his bodyguard McKinley Lee, and Snoop's friend Sean Abrams, who were charged with the 1993 murder of 20-year old Philip Waldermariam in West Los Angeles.

According to police, Snoop, whose real name is Calvin Broadous, was in the driver's seat of his black jeep on August 25, 1993, when an argument occurred between Abrams and Waldermariam, who were members of rival street gangs. Waldermariam was upset that Snoop and his friends had moved temporarily into his neighborhood while recording his album *Doggy Style* at a nearby studio. Lee, who was in the passenger seat of the rapper's car while Snoop was behind the wheel, testified that Waldermariam pointed a pistol at the car, forcing Lee to shoot Waldermariam in self defense.

The prosecutor, Deputy District Attorney Edward Nison, argued that Waldermariam was unarmed at the time of his shooting. Nison also pointed out that Waldermariam was shot in the back; this meant the slain man was either walking away from Lee or, at the very least, in a nonthreatening position.

Cochran and the rest of the defense team were steadfast in their belief that the shooting was in self-defense and had occurred only after Lee witnessed Waldermariam going for a gun in his pants. A point in the defense's favor was the accidental destruction of evidence by the police. The prosecution argued that the lost items, including shell casings and Walder-mariam's blood-stained clothing, were insignificant in the case. However, Cochran had scored points by uncovering mishandled evidence in another case he was involved with at the same time, and he was able to convince the jury that the missing evidence tainted the LAPD's case.

On February 20, 1996, more than two years after the three men were arrested and charged with the murder, they were acquitted of the murder charges. The jury took a week to deliberate, and remained deadlocked, 9 to 3, on the involuntary manslaughter charges, which were later dropped. Snoop, Lee, and Abrams were now free men.

This case was overshadowed somewhat by the "other" trial that Cochran was working on at the time, the one in which he had first pointed out the LAPD's mishandling of evidence. That case was the murder trial of former football star Orenthal James Simpson.

8

"IF IT DOESN'T FIT, YOU MUST ACQUIT"

❧

THE O. J. SIMPSON murder trial was one of the most closely watched trials in history. Day in and day out, soap operas, talk shows, game shows, and even a Presidential State of the Union address were somehow affected by the televised proceedings. The press quickly deemed it "The Trial of the Century."

On June 17, 1994, an entire nation had watched live as O. J. Simpson led an seemingly endless cadre of police cars on a low-speed chase along a major Los Angeles freeway. Earlier that day, he had learned that police wanted to arrest him for the June 14 murder of his ex-wife, Nicole Brown Simpson, and of her friend Ron Goldman.

The police had contacted O. J.'s lawyer, Robert Shapiro, on the morning of June 17, and told the attorney his client would be charged with two counts of first degree murder. At the time, Simpson was staying at his friend Robert Kardashian's house. Shapiro had gone to the house immediately, along with doctors and forensic experts who obtained samples of blood, hair, and skin tissue from the former star running back. Later in the day, the police showed up at Kardashian's house to arrest Simpson, but he was not there. He and a friend, A. C. Cowlings, had fled in Simpson's white Ford Bronco, leaving Shapiro to explain their absence to the police. Shapiro made a televised plea for O. J. to turn himself in.

O. J. Simpson tries on a pair of leather gloves found at the scene of his wife's 1994 murder. The gloves were too small for his hands, leading Johnnie Cochran to admonish the jury, "If it doesn't fit, you must acquit."

Millions of television viewers watched as O. J. Simpson's white Ford Bronco was pursued at slow speed by police cars down a Los Angeles freeway. Although Simpson eventually surrendered, his attempted flight convinced many people that he was guilty of murdering his wife, Nicole Brown Simpson, and 23-year-old Ron Goldman.

As Cowlings drove O. J.'s white Ford Bronco north on the 405 Freeway, the public was already judging him guilty in the brutal murder of his wife. Stories that he had a passport and disguise in the back seat, or that he was holding a gun to his own head, started to surface on television. Simpson's evasive and erratic behavior could only be that of a guilty killer.

Cochran, previously a casual acquaintance of O. J., watched the televised chase while providing legal commentary about the situation on ABC's *Nightline*. The chase came to a peaceful end when Simpson surrendered, but the lawyer knew this was only the beginning.

From jail, Simpson called Cochran repeatedly to join his legal team. Each call he left for Johnnie ended with a declaration of his innocence. Simpson's preliminary hearing came and went July 8, yet Cochran remained on the sidelines. Simpson, held over for trial, continued calling. Cochran asked friends for advice on whether he should take the case. Finally, he agreed to speak with the former football star. After hearing Simpson's story, Cochran believed he was innocent. He agreed to take the case.

Cochran went to visit O. J. in the lockup behind the Criminal Courts Building. The two touched hands through the wire mesh that separated inmates from their visitors, and O. J. expressed his deep gratitude toward Johnnie. This meeting apparently lifted Simpson's spirits. A short time later, when he appeared at his arraignment before Judge Cecil Mills, O. J. stood tall and told the judge he was "Absolutely, 100 percent not guilty."

The trial began in January of 1995. Gilbert Garcetti, who had been head of the special investigations department when Cochran worked in the DA's office, was now the district attorney. To present the prosecution's case, he appointed Marcia Clark and Bill Hodgeman. (An illness forced Hodgeman to leave before the trial was finished; he was replaced by Christopher Darden.) Cochran headed the defense, assisted by another well-known defense lawyer, F. Lee Bailey, and Simpson's attorney Robert Shapiro. A jury was selected, composed of eight women and four men. Eight members of the jury were black, one was white, one was Latino, and two were of mixed heritage. Judge Lance A. Ito would preside over the trial.

The prosecution wanted to prove that Simpson, who apparently had been physically abusive to his wife in the past, had overpowered her at home and stabbed her to death. When Ron Goldman, a waiter at the restaurant where Nicole and her children had just dined, showed up unexpectedly to return a pair of glasses she had left on the table, prosecutors claimed that Simpson also killed the 23-year-old in a jealous

Johnnie Cochran, as head of Simpson's defense team, was up against a formidable opponent in Marcia Clark, the lead prosecutor for the Los Angeles District Attorney.

rage. He then fled the scene in his white Bronco. Although there were no witnesses to the crime, the prosecution planned to produce clues, including traces of blood found at the scene and in Simpson's car, that proved that he was the killer.

Cochran's strategy was to prove that the prosecution was "rushing to judgment" in trying to convict Simpson. As a result, he felt, the police had neglected to pursue other leads. He also planned to prove that the police investigators had mishandled evidence and that several key clues might have been tainted by racism.

As the trial began, the prosecution attempted to establish the defendant's pattern of physical abuse toward his wife. Clark called to the stand the 911 operator who took a distress call from Nicole on New Year's Day 1989, complaining about O. J.'s erratic behavior. Another witness, Nicole's sister Denise Brown, also testified about Simpson's abusive and jealous behavior.

Cochran was more concerned about the testimony of Detective Mark Fuhrman, who had discovered some of the evidence that pointed toward Simpson's guilt. The defense team was looking into Fuhrman's background, to see if there was a hidden reason he would want Simpson locked away, but had not found much more than rumors yet. Cochran knew that everyone was expecting him to cross-examine Fuhrman, a white police officer, in a dramatic racial showdown, so he decided to throw off the defense by letting F. Lee Bailey cross-examine the detective. One question the shrewd defense lawyer asked Fuhrman would come back to haunt the detective, and the prosecution, later in the trial. "Do you use the word 'nigger' in describing people?" Bailey asked.

"No, sir," Fuhrman said dryly.

"Have you used that word in the past ten years?"

"Not that I recall."

"And you say under oath that you have not addressed any black person as nigger or spoken about blacks as niggers in the past ten years, Detective Fuhrman?"

"That's what I'm saying, sir," Fuhrman responded.

The prosecutors then called to the stand Richard Rubin, a former executive with a company that made gloves. A pair of gloves had been found at the murder site, and the district attorney wanted to prove that they belonged to Simpson. After Rubin's testimony about his former company, which manufactured the gloves, prosecutor Christopher Darden planned to ask O. J. to try them on, intending to surprise him.

Cochran and Simpson had talked about the gloves, and O. J. repeatedly told his lawyer that the gloves were not his. Now, Cochran silently hoped that Darden would try to trap O. J. with the request. Darden asked Simpson to stand in front of the jury and put on the gloves. Simpson did as ordered, struggling to fit the black gloves onto his large hands.

"They don't fit," Simpson said to Darden. "They're too tight."

As Cochran drove home that afternoon, he thought the defense might have just won the case.

After introducing several other pieces of evidence, Marcia Clark's prosecution team rested its case on July 6, 1995, six months after the trial opened. Now it was the defense's turn, and Cochran, Bailey, and Shapiro— nicknamed the "Dream Team" by the media—began attempting to discredit the evidence against Simpson.

First, Cochran had forensic scientist Michael Baden examine the coroner's description of the intense struggle that had preceded the killings. Baden explained in detail how facts collected at the scene did not support the prosecution's reconstruction of the murders' actual sequence. Another world-renowned forensic scientist, Henry Lee, testified about the LAPD's sloppy methods of collecting and preserving evidence. He explained how any error in the process of collecting and handling blood samples could render all subsequent evidence useless.

The next order of business was to destroy the credibility of Mark Fuhrman. By this time, the defense had become aware of a police department investigation into allegations that Fuhrman had a collection of Nazi paraphernalia. This could mean the detective had a racist motive to see Simpson behind bars. The LAPD's Internal Affairs (IA) division was also investigating rumors that Fuhrman had conducted an affair with Nicole Brown Simpson. The defense asked Judge Ito to obtain the results of the IA investigation, but because it was considered part of Fuhrman's confidential personnel file, the report was protected under privacy laws. Eventually, the IA report was turned over to Judge Ito, who deleted information he deemed irrelevant before handing it over to the defense team.

When Johnnie and his colleagues finally received

the records, there was nothing that showed Fuhrman had a history of racism or an affair with Nicole Simpson. Cochran had hit a roadblock.

Then, a defense team investigator, Pat McKenna, received a call from a lawyer whose client, a film producer, had interviewed Mark Fuhrman at length for a project. The producer, Laura Hart McKinny, was working on a script about the conflict between male and female officers in the Los Angeles Police Department. McKinny had hours and hours of taped interviews with Fuhrman, who was serving as her technical consultant. Cochran got in touch with McKinny's lawyers, who informed Cochran that the tapes would greatly benefit O. J. Simpson's case.

Judge Ito issued a court order, called a subpoena, for McKinny to turn the tapes over to him. At the time, she was teaching at a state film school in North Carolina. McKinny refused to submit the tapes. On July 28, 1995, Cochran and Bailey entered a packed North Carolina courtroom and requested that Judge William Wood Jr. enforce Ito's subpoena of Laura Hart McKinny's tape-recorded conversations with Mark Fuhrman.

The judge ordered the tapes to be played privately for him. Bailey and Cochran were also present, along with McKinny's attorney. The room grew silent as Mark Fuhrman was heard using vile racist and sexist language in casual conversation. In addition to his use of the slur "nigger," Fuhrman spoke about his disgust with interracial relationships. He also told McKinny how suspects are beaten by the police, how suspects are tortured to give a confession, and how evidence can be planted to ensure a conviction.

Judge Wood felt that the detective was playing a role for the film, and that these statements were not Fuhrman's true opinions. The judge denied Ito's subpoena. However, Cochran quickly appealed the ruling, and eight days later the North Carolina Court of Appeals unanimously ordered Judge Ito's subpoena to be enforced.

Back in Los Angeles, prosecutors Clark and Darden tried vehemently to prevent the tapes from being played in the courtroom. They even threatened to try to remove Judge Ito from the case, citing conflict of interest because Fuhrman had made some derogatory comments about Ito's wife, LAPD captain Peggy York, on the tape. The prosecutors eventually withdrew the threat. The defense attorneys gave Ito a list of 61 excerpts from the Fuhrman tapes that they thought the jury needed to hear. Ito allowed only two of the excerpts to be played. He also ruled that the defense could call Laura Hart McKinny, as well as several others involved in the film project, to testify about Fuhrman using racial slurs and epithets in their presence.

On September 5, 1995, the jury finally heard the two excerpts from the Fuhrman tapes. The next day, Fuhrman refused to answer questions about the tapes, citing his Fifth Amendment right of protection from self-incrimination. This battle had been won by the defense.

There was one more important decision that the defense team needed to make: should O. J. Simpson testify or not? If the former football star took the stand, he could speak in his own defense and tell the jury what had happened in his own words. However, the prosecutors would also have an opportunity to question Simpson. Cochran weighed the pros and cons of O. J.'s testimony, and decided not to put his client on the witness stand. His reasoning was that testimony by Simpson would extend the already-lengthy trial by several more weeks. The jurors were showing signs of fatigue, and Cochran didn't want additional testimony to overwhelm them. On September 22, 1995, the defense rested.

In her final argument, Marcia Clark reaffirmed the "ocean of evidence" the prosecution had presented; there was enough, she believed, to convict Simpson of the murders. Cochran and the defense team watched and waited as Clark reviewed the prosecution case

Discrediting the testimony of LAPD detective Mark Fuhrman was a key for the defense team. Cochran believed that Fuhrman had a racist motive for wanting to see O. J. Simpson jailed, and tried to prove that the detective had planted information to frame Simpson.

point by point. When she was done, the court broke for lunch.

At 1 P.M. on September 27, 1995, Johnnie Cochran arose from the defense table and began his final statement. He asked the jurors if they had ever been falsely accused of something, only to have their fate judged by someone else. Next, he addressed a specific point of the prosecution: that Simpson had disguised himself by wearing a knit cap the night he murdered his wife and Ron Goldman. Cochran reached for a knit cap, similar to the one O. J. had allegedly worn, and turned directly toward the jury.

"Let me put this knit cap on," he said. "You have seen me for a year. If I put this knit cap on, who am I? I'm still Johnnie Cochran with a knit cap. And if you looked at O. J. Simpson over there—and he has a rather large head—O. J. Simpson in a knit cap from two blocks away is still O. J. Simpson. It's no disguise. It's no disguise. It makes no sense. It doesn't fit. If it doesn't fit, you must acquit."

On October 5, 1995, at 10:07 A.M., the jury returned its verdict: "Not guilty." O. J. Simpson was acquitted of all charges and was finally a free man. Cochran's head fell onto Simpson's shoulder in jubilant relief, for he had once again rescued a client from what he believed to be the injustice of a corrupt police system rooted in racism. Yet, unlike other cases in which he fought against police abuses, this time the entire world was watching. The O. J. Simpson trial had been closely followed by the media, and millions of people actively followed the case's many developments.

Foreign response was mixed. Barry Wigmore, a reporter for the British tabloid *Today*, told CNN that most of his countrymen believed the American justice system was flawed. A short time later, his paper ran a five-page story on the verdict under the headline "What a Farce." In Germany, the verdict led news bulletins. In Brazil, one television commentator said, "What's really on trial is racism in the United States."

He was correct: never before had a trial so racially polarized the country. From the time O. J. was arrested, public opinion polls showed most blacks believed he was innocent and most whites judged him guilty. African Americans openly celebrated his acquittal, while white commentators, including Clark, Darden, and Fred Goldman, the father of slain Ron Goldman, blasted Cochran for introducing the question of racism into the O. J. trial.

The issue of race will continue to affect life in the United States. Some people felt that Cochran used an underlying distrust of police by African Americans to his advantage to get an acquittal with a jury composed mostly of African Americans. But Johnnie Cochran did not create racism, did not inspire police officers like Mark Fuhrman, and did not contribute to the history of police brutality against African-American defendants. Cochran has always felt that his duty as an attorney is to expose the existence of racism in the justice system and face it head-on, in hopes that one day all of America's citizens will be treated equally.

Cochran pulls on a knit ski cap during his summary remarks, to make a point about the prosecutor's assertion that Simpson had attacked his wife and Ron Goldman in disguise. "O. J. Simpson in a knit cap from two blocks away is still O. J. Simpson," Cochran told the jury. "It's no disguise." His remarks swayed the jurors, who acquitted Simpson of all charges.

9

THE LEGACY OF
JOHNNIE COCHRAN

❦

JOHNNIE COCHRAN JR. has gained fame for winning dozens of high-profile cases during his lengthy career. In his autobiography he mentions several cases that were most important to him. A majority involve abuses by police, such as the $2.4 million award for the wife and children of Yusaf Bilal, a 38-year old bus driver who was shot in the back and killed by a state highway patrolman during a routine traffic stop; $3.1 million for the widow and eight children of a 62-year-old disabled man who suffered a broken neck at the hands of sheriff's deputies while in custody for a misdemeanor traffic offense, then was left alone for five hours in a jail cell, where he died; $3.7 million for the four children of a couple killed when a West Covina police officer negligently crashed into their family vehicle; and over $1.5 million to the family of a 300-pound, 39-year-old barber who died of asphyxiation when police tied him up after he was arrested on suspicion of intoxication.

Another case that Johnnie is proud of is the multi-million-dollar settlement he won against the Los Angeles Unified School District after six girls were sexually molested by their teacher. The school district agreed to a $6 million settlement. Each of the girls would receive a payment, and about $1 million would be placed into a "special needs" trust fund administered by an insurance company. The victims

Johnnie L. Cochran Jr. holds a copy of his 1996 autobiography, Journey to Justice. *In addition to his thriving legal practice, the attorney keeps busy with a variety of other projects.*

would be able to draw money from this trust if they needed it for psychiatric treatment or therapy because of the abuse.

Cochran donated $250,000 of his fee from the settlement to the Los Angeles Family Housing Corporation, which helps homeless families secure housing. Johnnie and Dale Cochran oversaw the construction of 10 townhouse-style units that would be used to provide homes for families that had been homeless. The development was named after his parents: the Johnnie L. Cochran Sr. and Hattie B. Cochran Villa.

Among his cases are some that have forever changed the justice system and police department in Los Angeles. The high-profile cases of Ron Settles, Herbert Avery, and James Thomas Mincey Jr. led the LAPD to abolish use of the carotid choke hold. After the case of Leonard Deadwyler, Los Angeles County changed the way coroner's inquests are handled. Another change that stemmed in part from this case was the construction of a new hospital, the Martin Luther King/Charles R. Drew Medical Center. Many observers felt that Deadwyler's death could have been avoided if there was a hospital in his own neighborhood, and the McCone Commission, investigating the Watts riots, determined that a lack of access to health care had contributed to unrest. The commission recommended the creation of a new public hospital. King/Drew opened its doors in 1972, and today is the second-busiest hospital in Los Angeles.

Johnnie Cochran has been active in helping the African-American community in other ways as well. One of his most memorable achievements was a campaign aimed at curtailing the sale of chemicals used to make the drug phencyclidine, commonly known as PCP. A popular street drug in the late 1960s, PCP causes hallucinations and delusions. Because the drug's effects are unpredictable, users often become dangerous.

In the early 1980s, Cochran called for tighter

restrictions on the purchasing of the chemicals needed to manufacture PCP. These limitations would reduce supplies of the drug. He also pushed for stricter penalties for PCP use. His efforts, and those of others battling drug abuse in the 1980s, were successful; since 1983, use of PCP in the United States has dropped significantly.

Today, Johnnie L. Cochran Jr. is probably the best-known lawyer in the United States. He hosts his own television show on Court TV entitled *Cochran and Company*. The show features Cochran and a team

On his televised program Cochran and Company, Johnnie has interviewed many guests, not all in the legal field. Here, he tries on a hat given to him by basketball star Dennis Rodman.

of legal experts analyzing and debating the nature of the day's top legal stories, and the host also invites celebrities to discuss current issues. In 1996, he published his autobiography, *Journey to Justice*.

In addition to his television appearances and his law practice, in 1998 Johnnie Cochran somehow found time to launch All-Pro Sports and Entertainment, an agency he started with NFL agent Lamont Smith and Sean "Puff Daddy" Combs, president and CEO of Bad Boy Records. Smith already had a Denver-based agency that represented star running backs Barry Sanders, Eddie George, and Jerome Bettis, as well as a few dozen other NFL players. With Cochran on board, athletes need look no further than their own agency should any legal troubles arise. Cochran also plans to represent athletes interested in pursuing entertainment careers. In a June 1998 interview with Andre Taylor, Cochran said that he hoped to help young athletes avoid trouble. "I think clearly that is the one thing I want to do above anything else," he said. "I have seen athletes fall from grace [and] I am in a position to help them avoid some of these pitfalls."

In 1999, Johnnie became a partner in The Attwater Group. The group was developing Detroit's first casino, slated to open in the spring. And in February 1999, Johnnie's law firm opened a new office in Atlanta. The firm already had offices in Los Angeles; New York; Washington, D.C.; Dothan, Alabama; and Columbus, Georgia. Cochran also expected to open offices in Mississippi and New Orleans later in the year. A national law firm had been his dream for more than 10 years. The attorney also said that the firm would focus on personal-injury law cases, rather than criminal cases.

"When I decided to be an attorney, I admired the work of Thurgood Marshall and how he used civil law to change society," Cochran explained to the *Atlanta Tribune*. "In civil court, you can do so much more than in the criminal courts. In criminal cases, you defend clients' individual rights. It's you versus the Constitution. You're standing between your defendant going off to state prison or even the gas chamber. In civil cases, you can change individuals and the actions of institutions."

But Cochran's business interests have not taken away from his desire to see justice for all Americans. In 1998 and 1999, he became involved in litigation against the practice of racial profiling when he sued the New Jersey State Police on behalf of four young men in May 1999. The teens—three black, one Hispanic—were traveling through New Jersey in a Dodge van on April 23, 1998, when they were stopped by highway patrolmen. After being stopped, the van apparently rolled back toward the police car, and the policemen reacted by firing several shots into the vehicle, injuring two men sleeping in the back of the van and the passenger in the front seat.

Cochran insisted that the police stopped the driver, and reacted by shooting at the vehicle, because of racial profiling. He filed a civil rights lawsuit against the state police. "It's a very important lawsuit that hopefully will bring justice to citizens, not only in this region but across the country, as we focus attention on this burgeoning problem of racial profiling," Cochran told the media.

Johnnie Cochran has always wanted to make a difference for others. He wanted to make the judicial system work for citizens of every race; he wanted police departments held accountable for their actions. He has been successful, both from the inside as a district attorney, and from the outside, as one of this country's premiere trial attorneys.

With strength and perseverance, the world's most famous attorney continues to live the words championed by his late mother, Hattie: truth crushed to the earth shall rise again. No one can know the meaning of those words better than Johnnie L. Cochran Jr.

CHRONOLOGY

——— ✿ ———

1937	Born Johnnie L. Cochran Jr. in Shreveport, Louisiana, on October 2 to Johnnie and Hattie Cochran
1943	Moves with parents to California; Johnnie Cochran Sr. takes job at the Alameda Naval Shipyard
1959	Graduates from the University of California at Los Angeles
1960	Marries Barbara Berry
1962	Completes courses at Loyola University School of Law; takes position with the Los Angeles city attorney's office
1963	Admitted to the California Bar; becomes the first African American to hold the post of deputy city attorney in Los Angeles
1965	Leaves city attorney's office in March to work with Gerald D. Lenoir
1966	Leaves law practice with Lenoir to start private practice; meets Barbara Deadwyler, and takes on case of slain Leonard Deadwyler
1970	Defends Elmer "Geronimo" Pratt and other Black Panthers in the "LA Shootout" trial
1972	Unsuccessfully defends Pratt against charge of murder in the slaying of Susan Olsen
1977	Receives the Los Angeles Criminal Courts Bar Association's Jerry Gersler Award as attorney of the year; divorces wife Barbara
1978	Becomes the first African-American deputy district attorney in Los Angeles
1979	Initiates reforms in the district attorney's offices' procedures, such as requiring that a deputy district attorney and and investigator go to the scene of every police shooting; receives Law Enforcement Officer of the Year award from the California Trial Lawyers Association
1980	Founds Los Angeles County Domestic Violence Council; initiates reforms in the LAPD's Sexual Crimes Unit

1981	Returns to private practice, opening the Law Offices of Johnnie L. Cochran; takes Ron Settles case; the dispute is eventually settled out of court for $760,000, and eventually leads to a ban by the LAPD against the use of the carotid choke hold
1982	Appointed to the Los Angeles County Airport Commission by Mayor Tom Bradley; meets Dale Mason
1985	Marries Dale Mason on March 1
1989	Selected as Trial Lawyer of the Year by the Los Angeles Trial Lawyers Association; wins acquittal for actor Todd Bridges for murder charges
1991	Donates $250,000 to open Cochran Villa townhouses in honor of his parents
1992	Files lawsuit against the city of Los Angeles on behalf of Reginald Denny and three other victims of the rioting in the wake of the Rodney King verdict; wins $9.4 million award, the highest ever in a case of police misconduct, for a 13-year-old Latino girl assaulted by an LAPD officer
1993	Settles molestation charges against superstar Michael Jackson
1995	Leads the O. J. Simpson defense team called "The Dream Team"; named "Lawyer of the Year" by the *National Law Journal*; publishes autobiography *Journey to Justice*
1997	Helps Geronimo Pratt overturn his 1972 murder conviction
1998	Hosts *Cochran and Company* for Court TV; launches All-Pro Sports and Entertainment with Lamont Smith and Sean "Puff Daddy" Combs
1999	Files lawsuit against the New Jersey State Police, alleging racial profiling; opens office in Atlanta; joins Attwater Group to develop first casino in Detroit

FURTHER READING

Barovick, Harriet. "DWB: Driving While Black." *Time* 152 (15 June 1998): 35.

Cochran, Johnnie, with Tim Rutten. *Journey to Justice*. New York: Ballantine Books, 1996.

Cochran, Johnnie. "How Can You Defend Those People?" *Loyola of Los Angeles Law Review* 30 (November 1996): 39–43.

Corliss, Richard. "The Price Is Right." *Time* 143 (7 February 1994): 60–61.

Cose, Ellis. "Shuffling the Race Cards." *Newsweek* (9 October 1995): 34–35.

Cox, Gail Diane. "Who Ya Gonna Call? COPBUSTERS." *Los Angeles Magazine* (May 1991): 75–81.

Deutsch, Linda. "Judge Grants Bail for Geronimo Pratt." The Associated Press (11 June 1997).

Distad, Karl. "Profile: Johnnie Cochran." *Los Angeles Daily Journal* (15 September 1981).

Fischer, Mary A. "The Wrong Man." *Gentlemen's Quarterly* (March 1995): 202–209, 258–259.

Gleick, Elizabeth. "Coming to O. J.'s Defense." *Time* 145 (30 January 1995): 43–44.

Jervey, Gay. "Michael and Reggie's Magician." *The American Lawyer* (May 1994): 56–63.

Mitchell, John, and Doug Shuit. "Eulia Love: Anatomy of a Fatal Shooting" *Los Angeles Times* (16 April 1979).

Weathers, Diane. "The Other Side of Johnnie Cochran." *Essence* 26 (November 1995): 86–88.

INDEX

PICTURE CREDITS

COOKIE LOMMEL started her career as a journalist in the entertainment industry. She has interviewed hundreds of film, television, and music personalities as an on-camera reporter for CNN. Cookie has written two other biographies for young adults, on Madame C. J. Walker and Robert Church.

NATHAN IRVIN HUGGINS, one of America's leading scholars in the field of black studies, helped select the titles for the BLACK AMERICANS OF ACHIEVEMENT series, for which he also served as senior consulting editor. He was the W. E. B. DuBois Professor of History and Afro-American Studies at Harvard University and the director of the W. E. B. DuBois Institute for Afro-American Research at Harvard. He received his doctorate from Harvard in 1962 and returned there as professor in 1980 after teaching at Columbia University, the University of Massachusetts, Lake Forest College, and the California State University, Long Beach. He was the author of four books and dozens of articles, including *Black Odyssey: The Afro-American Ordeal in Slavery*, *The Harlem Renaissance*, and *Slave and Citizen: The Life of Frederick Douglass*, and was associated with the Children's Television Workshop, National Public Radio, the Boston Athenaeum, the Museum of Afro-American History, the Howard Thurman Educational Trust, and Upward Bound. Professor Huggins died in 1989, at the age of 62, in Cambridge, Massachusetts.